IMPRESSIONS OF INDIAN TRAVEL

IMPRESSIONS

OF

INDIAN TRAVEL

OSCAR BROWNING

GYAN

Published by

Gyan Publishing House
5, Ansari Road
Daryaganj, New Delhi-110002
Phone: 011-47034999, 9811692060
E-mail: books@gyanbooks.com

Distribution Network
gyanbooks.com
India, USA, Canada, UK, Australia, France

ISBN: 978-81-212-9338-9 (PB)
First Published, 1903

2nd Impression 2023

Printed at: Gyan Press, Delhi.

IMPRESSIONS OF INDIAN TRAVEL
AUTHOR: OSCAR BROWNING

IMPRESSIONS OF INDIAN TRAVEL

IMPRESSIONS

OF

INDIAN TRAVEL

BY

OSCAR BROWNING

LONDON
HODDER AND STOUGHTON
27, PATERNOSTER ROW
1903

TO

HER EXCELLENCY

LADY CURZON OF KEDLESTON,

AS A TOKEN OF

GRATITUDE AND RESPECT

FROM

THE AUTHOR

A month I lived in high romance,
In stately porch and columned hall;
Through rout and banquet, song and dance,
You were the beauteous Queen of all.

For India's star has many rays,
Many the pillars of her throne,
But the convergence of its blaze
Is concentrate on one alone.

Titania's spells are cold and dead,
Dividing, moans the sullen main;
Bottom has lost his ass's head,
And plies his weaver's trade again.

But still athwart his weary eyes,
Some flashes of unearthly light
Illumine, with a glad surprise,
The long, dull watches of the night.

OSCAR BROWNING.

King's College, Cambridge.

PREFACE

WHEN I was starting for India, a friend said to me, "You will write a book"; I replied that I should do nothing of the kind, that I was travelling for health and rest, and that I intended to give my pen a holiday. Another friend said, "You are going to India like Paget, M.P." When I reached Aden I received a letter from a friend highly placed in the Civil Service, containing some excellent advice. It said, "Do not think that you know as much about India as we do who have spent our lives in it; do not criticise our behaviour, and if you differ from us, hold your tongue."

I have written a book—or a sort of book—about India, but I hope that I have not proved a Paget, M.P., nor laid claim to any knowledge that I do not possess. I have written entirely as an impressionist, putting down on paper what occurred to me at the moment. Those who have visited India may like to see in print what they have felt themselves; and those who have not been there may wish to experience some of the emotions of one who has. Much of my time in India was spent in giving information about some questions which are now occupying the attention of the Government, and in discussing these questions with those most qualified to pronounce a judgment upon them. Obviously no considerations thus engendered have found their way into these pages.

I trust that my book, if it does not please,

will at least not offend, and that it may induce others to imitate my example, and to gather new experiences, perhaps at a more impressionable time of life, but certainly not under more favourable conditions than were vouchsafed to myself.

CONTENTS

The Voyage Out

1

I

THE VOYAGE OUT

TO leave the fog and frost of London, the frost and snow of Paris, the sleet of Marseilles, to sail upon summer seas, and to watch the dolphins and the flying-fish from an uncrowded deck, is a rare refreshment for a weary don. As day broke we found ourselves close to Elba and its satellite Pianora, and the majestic hills did not seem an unworthy sojourn for the emperor who once possessed them. Not far off was Corsica, his birthplace, with the gleaming bastions of Bastia and Piombino, his sister's appanage. Midday revealed to us Monte

Christo, at whose jagged and mysterious peaks I had often gazed from the Tuscan Archipelago. It lay now much nearer, and seemed worthy of its strange name and its stranger fate in romance. To-day it affords retirement to the King and Queen of Italy; it is here they shoot the moufflon, and recall the desolate crags of Montenegro.

The next day gave us Stromboli and the Straits of Messina. We passed close to the volcano, always active, on its picturesque side, with little Strombolino lying in front of it, as if a medieval castle had been shot, ready armed, from the crater, and had fallen into the sea to protect the town. The rest of the Lipari group stretched away into the haze. The passage through the straits gave us some hours of calm water, grateful to bad sailors. Charybdis was still turbulent, and to avoid her hidden reefs we steered close to the rock of Scylla, still bending her perfidious arm to catch the Phœnician trader and deliver his cargo into the hands of the wreckers. Few spots are more memorable in the history of the world. The Iapygian, the Phœnician, the Greek, the Roman, down to Nelson and Napoleon and Garibaldi, have here lost and won their fortunes; and now the tiny train is steaming out of Reggio, and the snows of Etna are looking down, as they have ever looked, unchanged amid myriad changes.

Christmas Day was spent out of sight of land. Next morning the rising sun tinged the snows of the Cretan Ida, and we traced the inhospitable southern shores of that long-drawn island, whose important towns lie all towards the north. On the following day the water grew quieter and greener, the sea appeared shallower, and was tinged with the muddy tribute of the Nile. We passed the Damietta mouth, marked by its lighthouse and its fishing boats, and reached our first stopping-place, Port Said. This harbour has an evil reputation ; but the novice in Eastern travel is easily satisfied. The town is not so very dirty, the air of the desert blows with an invigorating freshness, and the streets are thronged with every type of Eastern nationality. It is not unreasonable to take pleasure in a place even if you pity those who are obliged to live there. Here we had to coal, and did not start again till evening.

A great surprise awaited us. The sun had hardly set when we were enveloped in a dense fog. We crawled along with caution through the narrow passage, we ran on sandbanks, and got off with difficulty, and at last, in despair, we had to stop till daybreak. The oldest passenger had never seen anything like it. I suggested that it was an emblem of pushful Imperialism, and that the big Englanders were responsible for introducing the fogs of London into the Suez Canal and the chops of the Channel into the Red Sea. Still, every step of the way was interesting. The prettily decorated French stations, wandering Bedouin Arabs with their camels, lads like bronze statues diving for coppers, quarries filled with dusky workmen, London street arabs, not yet imported, turning catharine wheels on the shore, gave endless amusement; and above all was the clear sky, whitened with distant haze, and the sun, silvered by the sands of the desert, dropping to his grave.

Suez was nothing more to us than a row of lamps, and an emporium for postcards. About the middle of the Red Sea we had a storm which recalled to our Anglo-Indians their worst experience of the monsoon, and reminded us of the fate of Pharaoh. The waves swept the boat from end to end. Awakened by the noise, I came on deck, to find that we were passing through the group of ugly islands called the Twelve Apostles. The sky was cloudless and the stars bright, but the south wind was very strong. The next day things were quieter ; we saw the white walls and houses of Mokha, where the coffee comes from, passed the British island of Perim, with its flagstaff dressed to commemorate the proclamation of the Empire of India, threaded the Straits of Bab el Mandeb, the Gate of Tears, which separates Africa from Asia, and reached Aden at the close of the first day of the new year.

Here also the innocent abroad was fascinated by the diversity of Oriental types. Nothing is more beautiful than a Somali. His skin like dark lustrous metal seems incapable of motion till it moves, his carriage is dignified, his features are regular, and his expression intellectual and sympathetic. The Khaki-dressed Tommies were quite worthy of their position; they were grave and sensible, but were longing for home. Other signs of British rule were less impressive. Aden apparently once had a British benefactor named Briggs. When benefactor Briggs departed, the town determined to commemorate him, and they did this by enclosing a dingy promenade along the seashore, encircled by unhealthy plants kept alive with difficulty, and erecting in the midst a wooden bandstand, surmounted by crazy street lamps, the whole apparently purchased from a health-resort in liquidation. They added to this a commonplace gravestone, setting forth in plain English the virtues of Briggs. One turned with relief from this last word of Anglo-Saxon culture to the picturesque camel, ridden by a naked imp of darkness, to the cart drawn by prehistoric bullocks, to the comely features of our Somali guide, who, in his white dress, might have led Tamino through the halls of Sarastro. Imperialism may be strong, but it is not always beautiful.

Then came the Indian Ocean, with its sixteen hundred miles of bright blue water, exhilarating breezes, glowing sunsets, and nights lit by strange constellations, till the good ship *Salazie*, ever memorable for comfort, courtesy, and kindness, brought us to Bombay.

An Indian Train

II

AN INDIAN TRAIN.

WE reached Bombay at sunset, and, whilst making the long round which the entrance to the harbour necessitates, had opportunity to enjoy the beauty of the scene. Bombay is, as its name seems to imply, one of the great bays of the world. It is compared to the bay of Naples, but there is no Ischia, no Capri, and no Vesuvius. We lay in the roads all night, and spent four hours next morning before we were moored by the side of the quay. I can say little about Bombay, as I left it the same evening, but I hope to see more of it on my return. I can report that the offices of Messrs. Cook are very large and airy, and that the clerks are extremely courteous; but why they should, without question, send you to Calcutta round by Jabalpur, when the route by Nagpur is many hours shorter and ten rupees cheaper, is as yet to me an unsolved mystery. I can also say that the town of Bombay is redolent of Italy, and that the view from the balcony of Watson's Hotel into the square below is delightfully suggestive of that country, except that the trees, the birds, and the inhabitants are all different. I can certify that Government House is a fairy edifice, with a lovely garden, and an exquisite view of the bay from the drawing-room windows.

Even a few hours cannot be spent at

Bombay without a visit to the Towers of Silence, the grim burying-place of Parsees, where the tombs are living animals, and the vultures sit on the infected palm-trees, waiting patiently for their victims; or to the native town, where every step is a picture of character and colour, and where the mind is taken back through Pompeii to ancient Greece, and to the Arabian Nights.

It is forty-six hours' journey from Bombay to Calcutta, and these have to be spent in an Indian train, which for the benefit of destined travellers I may as well describe. The first-class carriages are roomy and lofty, the floor-space being, to speak accurately, twelve feet by ten. Each compartment contains four berths, and, as you are informed by an inscription, six seats, but you generally can have one to yourself, as I did. A convenient washing-room is attached, in which, if you like you can go to the length of having a bath. The native servant whom you have hired at Bombay purchases your bedding, for the journey—a mattress composed of two soft coverlets, sheets, blankets, and a pillow. A very little reflection will show you how much better it is that you should buy these conveniences new, than that you should use those which have already served for others. The carriages are not sufficiently well lighted to allow you to read with comfort, and, if they were, the jolting would render it impossible, as the track is not a model of perfection, and the dust is very trying. The best thing you can do is to sleep all night and to doze all day, gazing out from time to time at the strange sights which present themselves, as you move. You will then discover that a jungle is not a tangled forest, but any odd piece of waste ground; that tigers may abound in districts which seem little calculated to give them shelter; that natives always walk in single file, and that they are continually washing themselves, even in the dirtiest water.

The refreshment arrangements are admirable. Soda water is offered to you just as you are conceiving the wish for it; tea comes to you punctually at 6 a.m., and as often as you may desire it during the rest of the day. No sooner have you passed your hand over your stubbly beard than a barber appears to shave you in the carriage. You get a "little breakfast" of eggs and bacon, with bananas and oranges, at eight, a delightful tiffin in the heat of noon, and a good dinner at sunset.

2

Indeed, your wishes are no sooner conceived than they are satisfied as if by magic, "without rest and without haste," as the German poet sings. In this manner day succeeds night and night day, till you reach your destination, dizzy, but unfatigued. During the journey you have been rarely excited, but never dull. Perhaps the passage of the Jumna at Allahabad would have been the nearest approach to the first sensation, if it had not taken place at one o'clock in the morning; you also infer that Jabalpur is a fine city, although you may never have heard of it before. Benares you do not behold, as you are fast asleep in the darkness.

You have fellow-travellers who travel with you for a space: an active engineer from the Deccan, with a clear-cut face, anxious to know whether his chance companion is a relation of Robert Browning; a vigorous overseer from the coalfields dealing every day successfully with strange emergencies; a brawny Scotchman, strong as a giant and simple as a child, rushing off for his one-day holiday to the Calcutta races; he has made a pot on the Viceroy's Cup, and is now about to try his luck in the Metropolitan. The British in India work hard, and their relaxation is sport.

But the third evening has arrived, the day has hurried into night. My bearer has packed up my bed and bedding, the brawny Scotchman has collected his belongings, and has said "good-bye" to the spruce Baboo advocate in the next compartment, who is making a huge income by the litigious disposition of his countrymen. It is obvious that we are passing through suburbs; the train stops, and here is my oldest Eton pupil to welcome me on the platform, and the scarlet liveries of the Viceroy are gleaming among the dusky crowd.

Calcutta

III

CALCUTTA

WHAT am I to say about Calcutta? Utterly unknown to me when I came to India, it seems to me now so well known to all Englishmen that there is nothing left in it to describe. A city of more than a million of inhabitants, the capital of a great Empire, it is still formless, and presents a strange mixture of magnificence and squalor. The main feature is the Maidan, the flat plain which stretches from Government House to the banks of the Hooghly. It contains statues, a racecourse, a polo ground, cricket fields, a fort (even Fort William), a camp, and many other details worthy of notice. The Strand is the favourite drive along the banks of the Hooghly, where fashionable Calcutta disports itself every evening in quest of the southern breeze. The Eden Gardens, laid out by the side of the Maidan, have an English cricket ground, which carries you back to your native land. Cricket, I may say, is indigenous in India, whether it is played by the A.D.C. or the civil servant, by the white-robed Baboo or by the naked lad in an Indian village. The stumps, the ball, the bat are all of the approved English pattern, and the Baboo seems to think that his weapon will be more effective if it is thickly wrapped round with black whipcord. Besides these features there are the public offices, more useful than imposing; the Post Office, with many columns; and last, but not least, Government

House, the centre of attraction, its wings stretching out to every point of the compass, an emblem of the power which governs India so completely and so well. Perhaps, after all, the most striking building in Calcutta is the new Army and Navy Stores.

I used to think there was only one drive in Calcutta, that to Tolly Gunge, because fate always took me that way. It runs across the Maidan, past Belvedere, the home of the Lieutenant-Governor of Bengal, past the Zoological Gardens, over Zeerut Bridge, past the Palace of Warren Hastings, now renovated to receive native Princes who come to visit the Viceroy, home by Indian village communities—collections of small mud huts, destroyed every few years by rains, unconscious of the distinguished position which they hold in the theories of Political Science. This is the road which I always took, and the body-guard of the Viceroy seemed always to be travelling in the same direction. But after ten days I discovered that there was another drive, that of Bally Gunge, which leads to the lines of the Viceroy's body-guard, and passes more villages and more luxurious villas of Civil servants and merchants.

"Tros Tyriusve mihi nullo discrimine agetur."

I regard the two Gunges with impartial equanimity, and find little to distinguish between Bally and Tolly.

Tolly, however, leads to Khalighat, the most sacred religious centre of Bengal, one of the most sacred in all India. The temple, with an image of the terrible goddess Khali, who delights in blood, once human, now perhaps the blood of goats, stands on the banks of an old arm of the Ganges, and the name has been corrupted into Calcutta. It is the navel of the capital, and therefore the navel of India. The path to it is crowded with natives, and is extremely dirty. When we arrived, the principal door was shut, and we could only see the goddess through a side opening, and then not until her food had been changed. What we saw did not make us regret that it was only a glimpse, nor did the repellent features of an old hag of a priestess make us hanker after closer companionship. Behind the temple was a tree hung with bricks, and surrounded by strange offerings, even a thick tress of black hair lying under it. A Baboo, speaking mellifluous English, informed us that the offerings were made in hope of offspring. "Of course," he said, "we know that it is a superstition, but it is an old creed of our race." Khalighat is well worth a visit, and pilgrims crowd to it from all parts of India, sometimes stretching their length along for miles; but the sight of it does not enhance your ideal of Hindu religion, and reconciles you to the earnestness of missionary effort.

Some fifteen miles up the Hooghly is Barrackpore, once a large cantonment of British troops, now almost deserted because of the prevalence of fever. It is famous as one of the places in which the Indian Mutiny first broke out, but it is better known as the seat of the Viceregal Villa, where the Viceroy spends his well-earned rest at the week's end. The house is composed of lofty rooms, cool and shady, where the Governors-General could spend their summers in old days before the annual removal to Simla was invented. In front of the house grows a large banyan-tree, probably the largest in Bengal, except her more extensive sister in the Botanical Gardens of Calcutta. The tree protects with its shade a spacious dining-room, a drawing-room, a boudoir for Her Excellency, and a play-room for the children. Life is spent in the open air, breakfast and luncheon are taken under the awning of the Shamiana, and you loll all the morning in wicker-chairs, or play golf in the cool of the afternoon. The journey up the river is of unflagging interest. The mass of merchant ships in the pool is followed by the burning-places of the Hindus, where bodies may be seen cremating according to the most approved traditions of Greece and Rome. Stately ghats, or flights of marble steps, fringe the river on either side, leading to the garden houses of wealthy natives, or to Hindu temples, natives clothed or unclothed, with bright brass lotas, washing themselves in the stream, or drawing water which none but they would care to drink, give animation to the scene. The Danes, the Dutch, the Portuguese, and the French have left survivals of previous occupation, and Gallic Chandernagore is still permitted to retain an independent existence.

Another side of Calcutta life was shown to me by a performance of Shakespeare's *Coriolanus* in the original English, at Presidency College, by a company of native students. The pains taken to train the troop are difficult to realise and cannot be overpraised. It is much as if the A.D.C. were to give a performance of *Sakuntala* in the original Sanskrit. The critic might mark a want of originality, a stiffness of movement, and an imperfect accent; but the grouping was spirited and effective, and the English was better than would be spoken by an ordinary foreigner. Perhaps the most striking fault lay in the crude and garish colours of the proscenium and the scenery, showing that the Babu of to-day has little feeling for subdued and harmonious colour.

These stray and motley sketches are typical of the medley which Calcutta presents to the unaccustomed eye. The power and dignity of the Sovereign exhibited in its most impressive form, the rule of the Monarch imposed upon every detail of administration, the innate love of sport, equally necessary for the life of Englishmen and for supremacy over the native, the mixture of races, each with their peculiar dress and colour, united solely by allegiance to the British Crown, the picturesque incidents of life which make the charm of India, and above all the glowing sun, an enemy to be repelled by helmets and umbrellas, but the sovereign source of health and energy, supplying a groundwork of warmth and colour, and producing a climate which ensures that no one even in his most frivolous moments can ever talk about the weather,—all these things make up the first impressions of Bengal to the innocent abroad.

Darjeeling

IV

DARJEELING

NO visit to India could be complete without a visit to Darjeeling. It lies at the foot of the highest peaks of the Himalayas, so close indeed that the top of Kinchin Junga is only fifty miles off, and it scarcely appears more distant than Mont Blanc does from the village of Chamouni. Nor is the effect much more impressive. Kinchin Junga is over 28,000 feet high, only a few hundred feet lower than Everest, the highest mountain in the world ; yet the expanse of snow, visible even in January, is not so great in appearance as on Mont Blanc, because the rocks are so steep that the snow cannot lie upon them.

Let me give a more circumstantial account of the expedition. Leaving Calcutta in the afternoon, you reach the banks of the Ganges after dark. You cross the mighty river by a ferry-boat, and have supper on board. On the other side you find another train with the usual comfortable arrangements for sleeping, which are almost universal in India. Early next morning you find yourself at the foot of the hills, and you mount by a tiny railway with a two-foot gauge. You sit on a chair, and in seven hours climb 7,000 feet. I have heard some people pronounce the journey tedious, but it was not so to me. There was sufficient variety in the constantly changing scenery, in the richness of subtropical vegetation, in the marvellous construction of the line, following the sinuosities of the mountain road, curving round in single or in double loops, plunging boldly into jungle, switching backwards and forwards to reach a higher level. An American engineer who was with us said that it was the cleverest piece of workmanship in his line of business that he had ever seen. Ascending higher and higher, with less and less vegetation, and increasingly warmer wraps, we reach the summit of the line, near the village of Ghoom ; and, after turning a corner, the sunny town of Darjeeling comes into view, to which we descend in five hundred feet.

Darjeeling stands at the edge of a cliff with the giants of the Himalayas directly opposite, just as the giants of the Bernese Oberland rise opposite Mürren, only at a distance five times as great. The largest house in the place is the Shrubbery, the villa of the Lieutenant-Governor, the second is the palace of the Roman Catholic archbishop, and the third is St. Paul's School, where I was invited to stay. The Rector, as he is styled, is Mr. A. E. Newton, some ten years ago one of the most eloquent speakers of the Cambridge Union, hardly inferior to the great J. K. S. himself. Brought out to India by Bishop Welldon, in three years he has created an English public school in the heart of India. The boys wear Eton jackets, play games in flannels, and even submit to being flogged. These reforms were not introduced without difficulty, especially the last. An indignant parent wired, "Is it true that my son has had to remove his trousers in order to submit to corporal punishment?" The

Rector replied, "Perfectly true; results excellent." The telegram and the reply flashed like wild-fire over India, and the results were more excellent still.

The morning after my arrival gave us an unrivalled view of the great Himalayan chain. I will spare my readers the enumeration of names which I could not spell and they could not pronounce; suffice it to say that its most striking member, the Matterhorn of the range, a miracle of concentrated inaccessibility, is marked on the official map as D.2. Kinchin Junga is of course regarded as a god, and sacrifices are offered to him on Observatory Hill. Embers smoulder on the sacrificial altar, and lofty poles bear on high white banners inscribed with the prayers of the faithful. As the flags flutter in the breeze, the prayers ascend to heaven. The hillside is covered with these curious orisons, raised some in terror, some in gratitude, some to avert a dreaded landslip, some to thank the gods for a limpid stream of pure water. These mountain devotees are not less nature worshippers than the Greeks, and the rags which rustle over many a Cornish well may once have been inscribed with Celtic prayers. One day this sacred hill was occupied by British soldiers in a sham fight, and the shrine of the mountain god was profaned by the explosion of English gunpowder. Kinchin was not long in avenging himself. Next day a large part of Darjeeling was destroyed by a landslip, which has left many a warning scar on the hillside.

Next to the mountains, or, as they are curiously called by Anglo-Indians, the Snows, are the inhabitants, and no place is more favourable for observing them than the market-place on Sunday. There are Lepchas from Sikkim; Bhotians from Bhotan, a *terra incognita* to Englishmen; Nepaulese, straight, sturdy, and resolute; and Thibetans, with long pigtails, silken robes with broad sleeves, and round hats with turned-up brims, looking like Chinese with a difference, and redolent of the forbidden Lhassa. Willingly would I have asked the origin of each and have addressed them in their own tongue, but I could only gaze ignorantly and admire.

I secured some curios as trophies—a silver prayer-wheel, a box with a wooden handle, enclosing a scroll of Thibetan prayers, with a silver ball attached to its side by a chain. The worshipper turns the cylinder towards his heart—no easy matter—but to turn it otherwise is to curse, and, as he does so, he chants in a weird sing-song: "On mane padmé hum," which means "The jewel is in the lotus," the quintessence of the religion and the philosophy of Thibet. Some prayer-wheels have a round disc of ivory between the handle and the cylinder, and piety is measured by the number of discs the worshipper has worn through. Besides the prayer-wheel I have a jewel of strange shape, set with turquoises, and a very holy locket containing the ashes of a Lama mixed with cow dung. Mr. Sven Hedin tells me that these are all genuine, and that they were made in Lhassa.

Who ever goes to Darjeeling and does not ascend Tiger Hill? I rode up and down on a Bhotian pony, and the expedition lasted five hours. You pass through Ghoom, a native village, famous for a railway station, a tea-garden, a pig-breeding establishment, and a witch. Through luxuriant foliage you mount to the hill of Senchal, and then to Tiger Hill, a purely European name. On Senchal are weird traces of European masonry, of considerable extent, with pillar chimneys of weather-beaten brick, looking like the relics of a deserted monastery. No! These were English barracks, inhabited by English soldiers, who lived on this solitary height in the presence of the eternal snows, till the solitude and the strangeness ate into their brains, and one by one they threw themselves over the cliff and died. Their monument, a Runic cross, rises over the hill of Ghoom, and the cantonments are removed to Darjeeling. From the summit, Kinchin Junga, with his attendant peaks, towers more majestically than before; to the north-east stretches that long wall of rock, capped with snow and ice, unparalleled in the world, which shuts off Thibet from the rest of mankind ; and to the north-west are seen three little peaks, the farthest of which is Everest, the loftiest mountain of the world, the pinnacle of its roof. There is no doubt that this peak is higher than Kinchin Junga, because the sun tips it first, but there is a doubt whether it is the real Everest, that is, the mountain originally called by that name. At any rate, both have native names, more suggestive and more musical.

However that may be, let us ever rest and be thankful. We have seen the Roof of the World. We bid adieu to our hospitable friends, and we retrace our steps, the mountains veiled in mist, as if in mourning for our departure. We go down the hill more slowly than we came up ; we cross the sacred Ganges at sunrise, and are not sorry to bask once more in the sunshine of the plains after the penetrating cold of the heights.

Nimtola

V

NIMTOLA

EVERYBODY knows that the river Hooghly, on which the city of Calcutta stands, is a branch of the Ganges, and that the Ganges is a sacred river, on the banks of which every pious Hindu wished either to die, or to be burnt when dead, and have his ashes thrown into the holy stream. But burning requires wood, and wood costs money, so that in time it came about that the relations brought as much wood as they could afford, and that, when the supply was exhausted, the remains of the body were thrown into the stream, consumed or singed as the case might be. This committal of corpses to the Hooghly was an offence against health and decency, and was very properly put a stop to, and now matters are managed in a more orderly way.

There are three main burning-places on the banks of the Hooghly at Calcutta—Khalighat, the very sacred spot which I have already described, Nimtola, and a smaller place higher up the river. Of these Nimtola is the principal, and the bodies burned there average forty a day. The ceremony is most impressive. The body is carried, a few hours after death, by the relatives and members of its caste, wrapped in matting on a bamboo bed. On the floor of the burning-place, which is surrounded on all sides by walls, there are a number of shallow pits. The relations also bring logs of wood on their shoulders, which are carefully laid crosswise over the pit.

During this time the corpse has been lying at the side, covered with a new cere-cloth of pure white muslin, a portion of which has been torn off for the use of the chief mourner. Attendants, the duty of whose caste it is to wait upon the dead, remove the slight covering of the dead man, while he is still covered by the muslin sheet. The chief mourner now steps forward. He is the nearest male relative, in the case which I witnessed the son-in-law. He goes down to the Ganges with an earthen pitcher, and fills it with water. Coming back to the corpse, he sprinkles water over the muslin cere-cloth, and places some in the mouth and on the breast of the dead body. The corpse is then lifted on to the logs, and more logs are placed over it, so that the body occupies the centre of the pyre.

Now the chief mourner again comes forward, he takes the portion of the cere-cloth which has been retained for his use, and tears a small piece off it. He descends once more to the Ganges, and washes himself in the sacred stream; removing his loin-cloth or dothi, he girds himself with the new loin-cloth of muslin, which he must wear for a month as a sign of mourning. A plate of mixed ghee, incense, and sandal-wood is then brought to him. Moulding it up into a paste with Ganges water, he places some of it in the mouth of the corpse, and then washes his hands in sacred water, and dries them with the smaller piece of muslin which he has torn off.

Close by the pyre lie bundles of long

reeds. The chief mourner takes a handful, lights them, and places the fire in the mouth of the corpse. He then solemnly walks round the pyre, and the flame ascends. Five times does he make these peregrinations, each time casting his lighted reeds into the trench, so that the fire is well alight. His work is then done, and the earthen pitcher will be broken that it may not be used again. The open space outside is covered with the fragments of such pitchers. The bamboo bed also, on which the body has been brought, will be thrown upon the pile, and will explode with loud reports. In four hours the body will have been consumed, and the ashes will have fallen into the pit. A small portion of them will be thrown into the Ganges, and it is difficult to distinguish between the ashes of a man and the ashes of wood. The members of the dead man's caste, in this case the caste of the Kahars, or Bearers, stand round till the ceremony is complete.

Such is the system of cremation, as it has prevailed among the Hindus from time immemorial; as it prevailed amongst the Greeks and Romans. It has its roots deep down in the traditions of the Aryan race. To the sympathetic mind nothing can be more decent or more dignified. No offence is given to any sense, the eye sees nothing unseemly, and the scent of the pure fire fills the air. The corpse, with its dusky skin, does not shock as the pallid body of a white man might shock. There is no weeping or lamentation, but there is no indifference. The behaviour of the *haeres* and of the *gentiles* is solemn and decorous; they believe themselves to be in the presence of the dead man's spirit. The victims of plague and cholera alike find their destiny in the purifying flame; and the smoke which ascends above the walls of the enclosure tells not of some barbarous rite, but of the decent and wholesome annihilation of the mortal tenement which once held a beloved soul.

Perhaps less edifying is the Moribund House close by. When a patient has been given up by the doctors, he is brought down to the river, that he may die there and be immediately consumed. A paternal government has provided a lodging for these incurables; but doctors are fallible, and the death which they pronounce immediate often lingers. Yet to be carried back alive would be a dire disgrace. The old woman whom I saw huddled up on the stone floor had been dying for eight days. Let us hope that the girl who was watching her gave her enough to eat and drink. She cannot be carried home, but ghat-murder has been forbidden, and it would be criminal to hasten her end.

Native Life

VI

NATIVE LIFE

I HAVE lately had an opportunity of seeing something of native life. A lady brought up at Girton is married to the son of a distinguished Hindu, who has himself received an European education. They live in one of the most beautiful houses of Calcutta, an old palace of John Company, with spacious grounds, lofty rooms, and verandahs which form a mansion by themselves. The night I dined there, six Indian ladies were present in native dress, far more becoming, if I may so remark, than the affectation of European costume, as brown arms are not as comely as white when issuing from a silken robe. The lady whom I had the honour of escorting knows Cambridge as well as she knows Calcutta. After dinner there was a reception, attended by many Indian gentlemen, in a great variety of costumes, from the severely buttoned coat, like that of a High Church parson, to a robe undistinguishable from a Bedouin blanket. There was also some Indian singing, tender and graceful, but disagreeably nasal, presenting intervals strange to European ears.

The evening passed very pleasantly, but the male and female elements did not seem to mix. The ladies sat huddled up on a sofa together, while their lords and masters wandered about, entirely careless of their existence. Still they seemed happy enough. Our hostess was radiant with gaiety and good spirits. It is often said in India that mixed marriages between Europeans and natives are a failure. In the cases which have come under my personal observation they seem to be an entire success.

The Maharajah Sir Joteendro Mohun Tagore, K.C.S.I., is a well-known figure in Calcutta society. His family is not ancient, his position is that of a wealthy zemindar or landed proprietor, and he cannot claim to rank with such potentates as Holkar and Scindiah. But his family has been attached to the fortunes of the British Raj, and has risen by slow gradations till it has reached the highest pinnacle. He lives in two large houses in the most crowded part of the native city. The second of his mansions is called Tagore Castle, from its castellated character, and it has a lofty tower from which the best view of Calcutta is to be obtained. He has a large temple in the courtyard of his house, and he is supposed to pass many hours of the day in poojah, or divine worship. But all his devotion cannot restore to him the purity of caste, which was lost by an ancestor touching a dead body, or some similar misfortune. We drove to visit him through streets which a full-sized carriage passes with difficulty, encumbered, as they were, with bullock-carts and every kind of obstruction. After having been received hospitably both by father and son, we drove to the garden-house of another Rajah, of the Sinha family of Paikpara.

Our carriage was more magnificent than those of the Viceroy. A gorgeous coachman sat on the box, and two servants stood behind, prepared to jump off and run at the shortest notice, while they shouted at the top of their voices during our passage. In India one comprehends the utility of running footmen. In towns where the streets are narrow and encumbered, the roadways bad, and the corners sharp, it is necessary to have attendants who will pilot you through these difficulties, and a stout staff is by no means an undesirable weapon.

The garden-house of an Indian noble plays no unimportant part in his economical arrangements. It is here that he spends the hottest months of the summer, removing with all his household, which in the case of our host numbered three hundred persons. The villa resembles a good-sized Italian palace, with large halls, marble staircases, balconies and verandahs. It is well supplied with pictures and sculptures, perhaps not more atrociously misnamed than they would be in an English country-house. Behind the house is a large garden, and it was here that we were to be entertained. After visiting the flower-beds and the forcing-houses, under the guidance of Mr. Chatterjee, the most eminent florist in the neighbourhood of Calcutta, whose name is known throughout Europe, we arranged ourselves for tea upon the lawn. The ladies of the establishment were, of course, in the Zenana, well out of sight, although we probably caused them some amusement.

The Rajah then proceeded to photograph us, and the splendidly framed copy which he presented to me in state at Government House is now before me. On the left sits the Maharaj Kumar Prodyot Tagore, who represents Calcutta at the Coronation, clad in silken robes, dignified and handsome. Next comes the Paikpara, the Rajah's younger son, a lively, intelligent lad of fourteen, who is still at school, and happily not yet married. Behind, in the centre of the picture, stands the Rajah's eldest son, a comely young person of twenty summers, already father of a family. In front are seated the English guests, my noble self, and Mr. C. E. Buckland, secretary to the Government of Bengal. The picture is completed by the florist Mr. Chatterjee and the Baboo Kali Kumar Dey, a well-known figure in Calcutta, clad in a gorgeous robe.

After tea we were entertained by a company of Pathan conjurers, and then the chills of the evening warned us to depart. The garden-house of the Paikpara Rajah is more or less modernised, and its possessor is evidently proud of the fact. It is not so with the "Emerald Bower," the garden-house of the Maharajah of Tagore, which we visited a few days later. This is indeed a dream of beauty, although its owner is rather ashamed of it and intends to modernise it on the earliest opportunity. The house contains a number of really good pictures, a Murillo of no mean distinction, and a Northcote which was once hung at Carlton House. The garden also is unchanged. Who shall describe this wilderness of tangled charm? The Zenana has its own avenues and lakes, the male division its own sanctuaries. On a mound, surrounded by water, is the temple, once hung with costly embroideries, where the Maharajah's aged mother spent her days in prayer and contemplation. In the midst of a rocky labyrinth is a domestic chapel, covered with Sanskrit inscriptions, consecrated to the busts of the founders of the family. The Emerald Bower is worthy of its name, and we hope that Indian procrastination will long defer the date when these sacred groves will fall beneath the axe, when its impressive gloom will be dissipated, when some "Capability Brown" of India will transform this paradise of loveliness into the trim suburban neatness of Hampstead or Dulwich.

Government House

VII

GOVERNMENT HOUSE

THE greater part of my time in India was spent in Government House Calcutta, and it is therefore fitting that something should be said about it. It is undoubtedly the most important and conspicuous building in the city; its front court faces one of the busiest streets, and its garden stretches far down into the Maidan. As it stands, with its majestic staircase, in the view of every passer-by, its four wings spread out to the four corners of the heavens, it is a fitting emblem of, perhaps, the most complete example of concentrated authority which the world has ever seen. In this respect Calcutta can hardly have been surpassed by Salona and Versailles.

The house was built by Lord Wellesley at about the beginning of the last century, and admirably does it fulfil its purpose. It is said that there is not sufficient accommodation for entertaining visitors, bachelors having to be relegated to tents on the lawn, and that the guest-chambers are too spacious for convenience. Certainly in Lord Wellesley's time travellers to India were less numerous than at present, and probably the business of the Government required a smaller staff and less room. But for purposes of entertainment and representation, no building could be more convenient. It is said to have been modelled by a Government architect upon the plan of Kedleston Hall, Derbyshire, the ancestral home of the present Viceroy, and the masterpiece of Adam. But at Kedleston there are only two wings, while at Calcutta there are four, and the likeness is in other respects more superficial than profound.

The chief or northern front is approached by a lofty stone staircase, reaching down to the gravel, guarded day and night by troops of the body-guard with lances. This approach is not used except on special occasions, as when the Viceroy returns from tour, and is received in state by the heads of the Government and of society. It was also employed, on one memorable occasion, for the funeral of the Earl of Mayo, who was stabbed by a convict in the Andaman Islands. The usual entrance, as at Kedleston, is underneath the staircase, where there is a spacious carriage drive.

The building is of three stories, which resemble each other, the central portion consisting of two marble vestibules, divided by a long hall supported by columns. On the ground floor the vestibule contains the visitors' book, and is tenanted by large numbers of red-coated but dusky servants, the chief of whom, a stately figure, speaks English, to the great convenience of the guests. These domestics are generally squatting or asleep, but they rise reverently and salaam at your approach. The columned hall on the ground floor is always cool and shady, and the vestibule at the other end is the Viceroy's private entrance, opening on to the spacious garden. The gravelled space in front is often occupied by the mounted body-guard, waiting for the Viceroy to drive out, as it is quite unthinkable that the Viceroy or his lady should ever take a drive, except with the attendance of lancers. They are a splendid body of men, recruited from the whole of India, but they are sometimes a source rather of danger than defence. The rooms which were assigned for my occupation were also approached from this vestibule, and were underneath the Viceroy's private apartments. They consisted of an ante-room, a sitting-room, a bedroom, and, what is the glory of India, a luxurious bathroom, it being the habit of most Anglo-Indians to take a warm bath at least twice in the day.

Mounting to the second floor, we find a similar arrangement—two large apartments united by a central hall. The room over the entrance is used for breakfast and lunch, one or more tables being set out as the number of the guests demands. At the farther end is the throne-room, where levees and drawing-rooms are held, and which is generally used for dining. The golden throne under a velvet canopy is the elephant seat of Tippoo Sahib, but, whatever its historical interest, it can hardly be called dignified or comfortable. The large hall which unites these two rooms is the state dining-room, not too spacious for the banquets of sixty or eighty guests which take place every week during the season. The spaces behind the columns are occupied by busts of Roman Emperors, huge, clumsy, and inartistic, sent by Napoleon I. as a present to Tippoo, and captured by the English. The chandeliers also have a similar origin.

The state dinners are very impressive ceremonies. The guests assemble gradually, and are disposed round the room by the aides-de-camp. When everything is ready the aide-de-camp in waiting goes to fetch their Excellencies, who are announced as they enter the room, and are then conducted round the circle. Each guest is presented in turn, excepting, of course, those who are staying in the house. A procession is then formed according to the strict rules of precedence laid down by Government, and as the Viceroy enters the dining-room the band plays the National Anthem. The Viceroy's band holds an important position in the establishment, and is the best orchestra out of Europe. It is directed by a man of genius, and whether regard be had to the variety and high character of the programmes, or to the delicacy and refinement of the execution, it is unsurpassed in excellence. The National Anthem is again played when the Viceroy rises at the close of dinner to give the toast of "The King-Emperor."

The wing opposite to that in which the Viceroy's apartments are situated is taken up by drawing-rooms and a billiard-room, but on the occurrence of large parties the third floor is utilised. This is occupied by reception-rooms, especially a drawing-room, a ballroom, and a supper-room, so disposed that there is no interference with the ordinary arrangements of the house.

Two other portions of the palace remain to be mentioned. One is the council chamber, on the first floor, which, as well as the passage which leads to it, is hung with the portraits of former governors-general. Here the council of the Viceroy meets both in public and in private sitting; here also are held the conferences, which have so usefully distinguished the reign of the present Viceroy. Far away from this in the distant angle are the Viceroy's own apartments, where the work is done which controls the fortunes of 294 millions of subjects. An aide-de-camp in uniform occupies the ante-room ; there are rooms for the secretary and his subordinates, and in the centre is the vast chamber from which India has been governed for a hundred years. If no ruler has more power than the Viceroy of India, few have harder work. Besides countless interviews, each of them of great importance to the chief and his subordinate, and the transaction of routine business with the secretaries of the departments, every day some thirty or forty matters of government have to be disposed of, large bundles of papers read, and when a decision is come to the reasons must be recorded in writing. The Viceroy's work begins as soon as he wakes, and is continued far into the night. It is only by knowing more about a question than any one else that a ruler can preserve that supremacy in council which is the mainspring of efficiency.

From the farther end of the Viceroy's room rises a staircase which leads to the third floor, where dwell his children and the lady who is the guide and comfort of his life. Her work is also very hard, and the demands upon her tact and judgment are continuous. But labour has its reward, and it may be doubted whether any of those who have swayed the destinies of India have planted themselves more firmly in the hearts of the people than the present occupants of the Viceregal throne, Lord and Lady Curzon of Kedleston.

Ghazipur

VIII

GHAZIPUR

GHAZIPUR is a settlement with a history. It lies on the Ganges, and it was once a frontier post. Hence it possesses large barracks and a bandstand, and a monument to Lord Cornwallis, who, going out to India in advanced years for a second time as Governor-general, succumbed to the climate within a few months. It is the centre, or one of the centres, of the opium manufacture, but the oblivion which that drug induces has had its effect upon the place, and it is unknown to the ordinary tourist. I should not have gone there except to visit an old friend and pupil, a Brahmin of high caste, who some years ago gained the first place in the Indian Civil Service competition, being first in nearly every subject which he took up. I was anxious to see my old friend, now married to a Brahmin wife of even higher caste than himself, and the father of two dark-eyed little girls, and to ascertain how he was prospering as an administrator, because when he obtained his distinction Professor Max Müller wrote to me that it was all a mistake, that he had better surrender the appointment and go to the Indian bar. I found him happy and prosperous, very laborious in "camp," which is the name in India for the periodical tour which all officials take through their districts, liked and respected by his European colleagues.

The problem of admitting natives to the Civil Service is a difficult one, but it is impossible to exclude them so long as the appointments are given by unrestricted competition. If they ever came to form a considerable portion of the service, inconveniences might arise, but it is improbable that under any circumstances they would ever form more than five per cent. of the whole. Their existence, thus limited, may be considered an advantage. They mitigate the grievance of foreign rule, and they have their peculiar use. However much an Anglo-Indian may assert that he understands the natives better than the natives understand each other, it is difficult to give credence to the conviction. A native of first-rate ability, who has been educated in England, must be a useful intermediary between the extreme divergences which characterise the Oriental and the Occidental mind. He must necessarily be able to understand and to assuage discontent, to expound the methods of English government, and even to give useful advice to his colleagues.

If I were a collector with a native assistant under me, I should frequently consult him and give great weight to his opinion. Even if it be true that a Bengali, however gifted, would not make an efficient frontier chief in a tight place, there is no reason why he should be put into positions which he is not suited to fill. Bengalis make excellent judges, and if the Indian Educational Service became a branch of the Civil Service would make admirable professors. What would happen if the more sturdy races of the north were to take to study instead of sport, it is needless to speculate upon.

My friend met me at the branch station on the Ganges. We crossed the river in a small steamer, and found ourselves in the city of Ghazipur, the cantonments being at a considerable distance. He drove me in European style, in what I suppose was a "buggy," or a "tum-tum," as I have never heard an Indian gig called by any other names, nor have I ever seen a buggy in Europe. The English cantonments are pleasant places, containing good roads, excellent for cycling, luxuriant trees, and spacious bungalows, and if it were not for the strange fauna and flora, not unlike a prosperous English village. After "tiffin," the universal name in India for lunch, I expressed a wish to see some Indian villages, and we went through the three which were nearest to my friend's house.

The Indian village community holds a

great position in the world of political science, but to the traveller's eye it is a collection of mud huts, with their blank walls turned outside. All that you see is a tall bamboo with a flag upon it marking the residence of the head-man. It looks as if everything interesting went on inside. Every village has a head-man, and I have little doubt that the inhabitants represent a kind of clan descended from a real or supposed common ancestor. I shall continue in any lectures that I may give on the subject to speak of the Indian as he is described in the works of Maine and Baden-Powell; but I can believe that personal inspection of many Indian villages might reveal varieties which would prove a hindrance to profitable speculation.

The villages which we saw bore the names of Kurtha, Hathi, Khana, and

Hospital, and they were all different in character. The village called Hospital, from its occupying the site of the military hospital, which existed when Ghazipur had many soldiers, was grouped around the tomb of a very holy saint. The inhabitants were all servants or devotees of the saint, and had a conspicuous mark on their foreheads to show that they were such. The temples, which we were not allowed to enter, were poor and squalid, and reeked with the odour of sanctity, but the youthful Ions seemed quiet and inoffensive.

The village was not a large one, and we did not visit it in a season of poojah. There may be times when the possession of the saint's ashes is a source of revenue to the proprietors. At any rate a village entirely occupied by the devoted worshippers of a dead holy man, who seemed contented and even honoured in seeing that and nothing else, was soothing to the European mind, and certainly could not be paralleled in our country. It is scarcely probable that the village of Hawarden will ever be occupied exclusively by a race of people engaged in the service of St. Deiniol's library, with the letters G.O.M. inscribed in vermilion upon their foreheads.

The next village was more typical. It was large and prosperous. The inhabitants belonged to the warrior class, and rather fancied themselves. We were met at the entrance by a strange mill for pressing sugar-cane—the trunk of a tree drawn round obliquely in a socket by two lovely and skittish bullocks, who became so unruly that they were removed in order that others more capable of being photographed might be substituted. I gazed long at the unwonted sight, soothed by the creaking of the mill as it turned, and the foaming of the molasses in the earthen pot. In the heart of the village sat the village potter, turning out vessel after vessel, according to his fancy, from his large horizontal wheel, recalling the agnostic utterances of Omar Khayyam. The larger pots had naturally no bottoms, and these were deftly supplied by the potter's wife, who sat by his side and supplied the deficiency with weird adroitness. Each village keeps a potter of its own, and he is apparently turned on to labour when the supply of pots runs short. The other streets were full of men, boys, and children, mingled with picturesque but obtrusive kine; and ever and anon a little girl peeped out from a doorway, with a red mark between her eyes, and I was told that she was a child-wife.

The village which last we visited was dwelt in by Mohammedans. It lay at some little distance, surrounded by beautiful trees, but it was small in size, and the inhabitants did not seem to be at home. If Indian villages, taken at random, are like these three, one can imagine that there is not much communication between them, and that the English have only to divide and govern.

After paying our respects to the memory of Lord Cornwallis, and dining in European style, I resumed my travels, my old pupil giving me the inestimable benefit of his company. He took with him a lantern, like the man in the moon, and a large porous jug of boiled and filtered water, both necessary for the safety and comfort of our journey. I left the Indian villages to their slumbers, wishing that I had seen many more of them. About midnight we reached Benares.

Benares

IX

BENARES

THE Ganges is the holiest river in India, and Benares is the most sacred city on the Ganges. It is here that the pious Hindu would wish to die and to be burned and to have his ashes cast into the atoning stream. Benares is one of the most ancient and populous seats of the Hindu religion. If Buddha came there, it is said that he expected to find on that spot the largest number of convertible people. It contains at least one shrine for every important deity of the Hindu theogony, from the wise Ganesha and the playful monkey to the clumsy giant, the Indian St. Christopher, and the bloodthirsty Khali. The streets swarm with temples, the river with bathers; and the city is also the focus of the learning of Asia, where Sanskrit is studied almost as a living tongue, although report says that its votaries are fewer and less profound than of yore. To the traveller, Benares has at least three aspects, to which the English cantonments may be reckoned to add a fourth.

The town lies at a considerable distance from the military station, which is rural and picturesque, as is often the case in India. The streets of the suburb are rich with Oriental variety, the houses are of stone and are more solid than the evanescent shanties of Calcutta. Bookshops also are more frequently found. When we enter the city, we find ourselves in a dædal of streets, as complicated and as bewildering as the calli of Venice. Take a guide, or you will be lost; take a guide, or you will be beset by the importunity of a hundred. You must visit the ancient observatory, built I know not when, and serving I know not what purpose; but it is obvious that he who made it was no mean mathematician, and thought the labours of wrought-stone spent to good advantage in the watching of the stars. The sundials remain, but the instruments have disappeared, only their massive sockets testifying to their size and complexity.

More interesting, perhaps, to the unscientific layman, is the view of the river from the observatory terrace. Here for the first time is spread out before him that holy reach, the cynosure of the hopes and the yearnings of devout India. We descend again into the labyrinth. There are shops full of Benares toys, wooden toys, lacquered and varnished and painted with bright colours, nests of boxes turned with exquisite skill, brass toys, equally well finished, lotas and dishes and statues of the gods; there are also representations of the lingam and of Buddha's feet. But the art of Benares is not in toys alone; its metal work is famous throughout India, and its silk embroideries rival the looms of Delhi and Cashmere.

Then the temples! The complexity of the Hindu religion is confusing even to a native, and to the foreigner it is unintelligible. The gods of Greece and Rome are represented, at least, as typifying some quality of the human mind, some longing of the unsatisfied soul; but a Hindu would find some difficulty in saying why he worships one divinity more than another, except that its sacred sign was marked upon his forehead at his birth. For this reason Hindu shrines are not very interesting to the uninitiated, although they might become so upon further acquaintance. Some are more, some less, noisy than others, some are disfigured by blood and filth, some you are allowed to enter, some you may hardly look at.

The so-called Golden Temple, with its roof covered by the lavish gilding of enthusiastic devotees, is rather disappointing. To the eye of the ordinary traveller the grotesque predominates. But it is not so with the worshippers. They pass you in the street, stalking onward with steady stride, as they have stalked for hundreds of miles, bearing strange burdens upon their shoulders, wreathed and crowned with marigolds, oblivious of your presence, and of everything else excepting the goal to which they are pressing, and which they have so nearly attained. There is nothing repulsive in them ; the most callous observer must be touched by their devotion as they chant in monotonous measure their creed of faith. No one can weary in watching these devotees and in wishing for equal faith in whatever religion he may profess.

The worshippers are hastening to the river, and to the river you must direct your steps. You find a boat at a convenient wharf, and you sit not in the usual manner, but in a chair placed upon a raised platform. You pass slowly down the stream and up again, watching your brother globe-trotters engaged in the same occupation, like them kodaking as you glide. "The Ganges at Benares in the early morning" is the *mot d'ordre* of Indian tourists. There is much that I cannot describe, but which has been represented more or less faintly in pictures—the towering buildings, the multitudinous steps, the richness and variety of colour.

Benares is a city of palaces as it is a city of temples. Most Hindu potentates have built castles on the Ganges, which rise aloft in various stages of architecture, some more commendable than others, but all picturesque. Connected with these palaces are ghats—that is, flights of steps down to the river for the convenience of bathers Of these the river is full, and you have an opportunity of observing at once the grace of the Indian form, the completeness and also the absolute decency of Indian bathing. The most careless observer must be struck by the substantial delicacy and purity of the Hindu mind. Little clothing is required, but the minimum is severely and fanatically exacted. Some women keep purdah even in the bath, and wash themselves under a linen tent; all are completely dressed. Long hours might be spent in observing their ablutions and estimating the happiness of those who are able to absolve themselves in that divine stretch of water twice in every day.

Then there is the burning, reverent and decorous, not enclosed within a wall as at Nimtola, but open to the stream. A dead Indian is but a little object when wrapped in a linen cloth and carried on a bamboo frame, and its passage need not make you shudder. I do not know from what distance they come, but large stacks of logs await their coming. There is nothing to disgust or to offend, only the piety of the mourners to envy and to admire.

Passing down a Benares lane, I saw a crowd of little boys in a side alley, and found myself in a school. I was courteously received, and ascertained that the children were being taught Hindi and English. All was carried on in the open air, apparently in a public thoroughfare, but there was no lack of industry, no need of enforcing attention. I was treated with the confidence which was due to a brother teacher: copy-books were brought to me written beautifully in English; sentences were read out to me which I could not deny that I understood; the Hindi writing seemed to me as neat and perfect as the English, and I was deeply impressed with the learning of Benares. I would willingly have spent two months where I could only spend two days.

Let him who loves the gliding of an

opalescent stream, the reflection of palaces in its waters, the glint of myriad colours on its banks, the sight of a nation seeking purity in that which it deems most pure, go to Benares. Let him also who respects the worship of the unseen, whatever form it may take, who is touched by the subjection of the material to the spiritual, and is impressed by the belief that the intellectual and the spiritual life are connected by indissoluble bonds, visit that sacred city, watch, reverence, and imitate.

Sarnath

X

SARNATH

MY Brahmin friend was much interested in Benares, and very helpful in interpreting the *genius loci*, but he attached still more importance to a visit to Sarnath, where some strange ruins are to be seen. We drove out in the afternoon for some miles through a pleasant and cultivated country, until we reached the objects of our expedition. They consist of two ruined towers. The first, which much resembles a Martello tower on the Sussex coast, is easily ascended, and there is a charming view from the top, with Benares in the distance, and a singularly green and English-looking landscape all round. If I had not gazed too narrowly at the character of the trees, I might have imagined myself in my own country. The other tower is about half a mile distant, and we were given to understand that the whole of the intervening space was once occupied with buildings. This second edifice is in the form of a truncated cone, and cannot be ascended; it is covered with elaborate ornamentation, now sadly disfigured by faults in the masonry.

To one standing at a little distance it was easy to see that the motives of the ornamentation were decidedly Greek. There was one row of a flowing acanthus ornament and another of a modified key pattern. In the museum which is attached to the tower there are many statues which bear evidence of Greek influence. The Viceroy has just created a Directorship of Archæology, whose work is much needed in India, where the reigning authority on the subject is the Public Works Department, generally known as the P.W.D.

The holder of this new office is a distinguished classical scholar, who has been thoroughly trained in the latest practice of archæology, having superintended excavations both in Greece and in Crete. The Indian Press clamoured loudly because the Government had not chosen an Oriental scholar, and one who had made his mark in specially Indian investigations. But any one who visits India with an intelligent eye will see that the India Office was right. Indian languages can be easily acquired by a classical scholar. There is a living scientific school of classical archæology, but there is no corresponding school of eastern archæology, while it is of the first importance to trace the connection between Indian art and the more developed forms which characterise the efforts of other Aryan nations.

The chief interest of Sarnath for me lay in the fact that it had been for a long time the residence of Buddha, certainly one of the most admirable personalities of history. He apparently came to this place because it was already a flourishing centre of Hinduism, and he was likely to find here an abundant crop of converts. Around the towers stretch far and wide heaps of brick and rubble, remains of ancient buildings. Indeed, Sarnath is the mother of Benares, as Benares is the port of Sarnath—her avenue to the holy stream. The whole region has been sanctified by the prayer and devotions of long generations of mankind, stretching out into a hazy past. The ruins also conveyed to my Bengali Brahmin friend evidence of the former spiritual and material predominance of Bengal; how, I do not precisely know, but the reflection was very consoling to his mind. There are some things which even the most conscientious globe-trotter cannot be expected to understand: one of these is the complicated ramifications of Hindu mythology, another is the exact relations which exists or ought to exist between Brahminism, Buddhism, and Hinduism. Let those who are conversant with these subjects forgive the ignorance displayed in these letters, and send me corrections for a second edition.

Sarnath also contains a Jain temple, severe, elegant, and impressive, as Jain temples always are. We were not allowed to enter, but we gazed from afar into the shrine. No one who visits Benares should omit to visit Sarnath. We lingered so long over the memorials of the past, that the sun had neared its setting before we left. India has no twilight, and we were soon left in darkness. The night was spent in an Indian hotel, of which the less said the better. The next morning, although we were to start early, the spell of the Ganges was upon me. I rose with the dawn, galloped down to the city, and lost myself once more in the maze of streets. I met the long procession of pilgrims, travelling for countless miles, bearing their strange burdens, and chanting their weird songs. I saw once more the bathing-places and the burning-ghat, and took my last look at the incomparable Ganges, illuminated by the rays of early morning, seeming scarcely to glide beside the sacred city, opaline and unruffled, enticing alike to the heated traveller and to the seeker for eternal rest. The Ganges is worthy of all the worship which has been paid to it, and he who has once been conquered by the fascination of its waters will not cease to yearn for them so long as he lives.

Secundra

XI

SECUNDRA

IT is a far cry from Benares to Agra. You find in the two places a different country, a different population, a different religion. In a sense, Delhi and Agra (and they may be taken together) are the capital of India—the capital, that is, of the Moguls, the Mohammedan sovereigns of the country, and of the Hindus who preceded them. It is the country of tombs and mosques, of fierce heat and bitter cold, and above all of masterpieces of art, which rival anything that Europe can show. Leaving Benares in the morning, we did not reach

Agra till midnight on the following day, and the Lord knows when we got to bed.

My Brahmin friend, although far from Hindu Bengal, was still in his element. His hero was Akbar, his aversion Aurungzebe. Akbar did his best to reconcile the two religions, and established a large degree of religious toleration; Aurungzebe was a fanatical, iconoclastic Mussulman, who persecuted the Hindu and cut off the heads of Akbar's stone elephants, because they represented animal life. If there had only been a race of Akbars, thought my friend, India might have been an independent Empire, and the necessity for the British Raj would never have existed. But Aurungzebe by his reckless intolerance spoilt everything.

It was in this spirit that we went to visit the tomb of Akbar at Secundra, a few miles from Agra. These huge Mohammedan tombs are strange things. The Koran, I am told, forbids tombs altogether. The body is to be laid simply in the earth, without even a stone to mark its place. How these exact provisions have been perverted into a system by which the corpse of a dead Mohammedan is installed not only in a palace, but in a compound, not only in a house, but in a garden or a park, I must leave a Moslem to explain. Perhaps they wish to emphasise the difference between themselves and the Hindus, who burn their dead and scatter their ashes. Perhaps they sin out of pure naughtiness and disobedience, and chance the punishment of the next world for the certainty of leaving a memorial behind them in this. At any rate, Christians may rejoice at their transgression, for if they had not disregarded the law, the Taj Mahal, the tombs of Secundra, and many other precious monuments would never have come into existence.

The actual tomb of a Mohammedan is of very moderate size, just large enough to hold the body, and he is not buried in it. Far down in the crypt, covered only with earth, or with a shapeless mass of rubble, lies the body of the king or the saint; the tomb high aloft, enriched and enhanced in beauty by all the efforts of the purest art, contains nothing or contains his ghost. Therefore the temple might be held to inshrine not the ashes, but the spirit of the dead. It is at once a record of piety and affection from the living, and a beacon to posterity of virtues to be emulated and passion to be revered.

The tomb of Akbar, like others of its class, is entered by a gateway, which leads into a garden, at the other end of which is the tomb itself. The character of the architecture is nothing if not symmetrical; it possesses none of the variety and richness of the Gothic, and little of the grace and harmony of the Greek. Mohammedan architecture does not show well in photographs, pictures, or models; it has the appearance of being mechanical. The outlines do not charm the eye as do those of the Parthenon or the Madeleine, and details which are beautiful to a nearer gaze are not visible in a general view. They must be seen and closely examined to be understood and appreciated. But when once seen and studied they produce an effect which is never forgotten.

In the tomb of Akbar you mount from the crypt, glowing with lavish colour, to the middle story, and thence to the roof, on the centre of which the tomb reposes. At its head stands a tiny pillar which once held the Koh-i-noor. The eye admires the exquisite stone fretwork and the lovely pavilions which adorn the angles. The whole building is decorated with those flowing characters of Arabian writing, easy to read by those who are acquainted with the character, if not with the language which has generated our title of Arabesque. The Arabian alphabet and the Persian, which closely resembles it, differ from other alphabets in the fact that every character is a personality. Treated as such, each character is capable of very wide modification, so that it forms an admirable means of adornment without losing its clearness for literary purposes. Nothing can exceed the beauty of these majestic flowing forms, clear as the day when they were first cut preserved in their original brightness by the Indian sun and cleansed by its summer rains. The vaults on which the building stands are enriched with bright mosaics, some of which, carefully and judiciously restored, are a witness to the former magnificence of the whole. In the hands of the present Viceroy and his director of archæology there is no fear lest these masterpieces of art will be allowed to decay or to fall into neglect.

Secundra contains other interesting monuments beside the tomb of Akbar; indeed, the whole road from Agra is bordered with tombs which recall the Via Appia at Rome. The most interesting are a tomb of red marble, standing at a little distance, rich with mosaics, but in a sad state of disrepair; and another tomb which is supposed to have been erected to a Christian Portuguese wife of the Mogul Emperor. This last now belongs to an English orphanage, and as our visit was paid on a Sunday, we had some difficulty in obtaining admission. Having climbed over the wall, and stirred up the presiding Padre from his siesta, we were shown over the place with great courtesy. The tomb, which is of very simple construction, contains schoolrooms and a printing-press, while the little orphans looked very happy and well cared for. The Padre told us that the most diligent search had failed to reveal anything of a tomb or a body; so that the destination of the building rests upon tradition. Its artless massiveness marks an interesting stage in the evolution of Mohammedan art.

The Taj Mahal

XII

THE TAJ MAHAL

ANGLO-INDIANS are most excellent people—perhaps no finer specimens are to be found of the English race; but culture is not their strong point. They do not, as a rule, read books, nor do they care much for music or for art. They very seldom possess a library, and they usually prefer a rousing patriotic ballad to a song of Schumann. But there is one work of art in India which they are all agreed to admire, and that is the Taj Mahal. It is the high-water mark of the artistic worship of every civil servant, and of every officer.

Each one of them has his own peculiar views about it. These are not concerned so much with the style of its architecture, or with its relation to other buildings, as with the manner in which you ought to see it. Here you should take your first view—here your last.

There are even schools of doctrine as to these matters, there are morningites and eveningites, moonlighters and middayers, but they are all agreed that the Taj is the one incomparable building in India and in the world; and if it ever occurs to them that the keenness of their own æsthetic susceptibilities has been a little blunted by the effects of their work and of the climate, they pull themselves together, even in their old age, and say, "At least I love the Taj."

The Taj is, indeed, one of the few works

of art, which, however familiar you are with it from photographs or copies, however jaded you may be with its merits from indiscriminate praise, does not disappoint. It pierces through every plate of your armour of preparation, and subdues you into new wonderment. For myself, I have been familiar with the Taj from my earliest years. The Fitzwilliam Museum at Cambridge devotes the whole of one of its rooms to housing an ivory model of the Taj on an enormous scale. The result is that you know of its existence and of its proportions, and you make up your mind that you will see it one day if possible. But you do not admire it. Its primness and symmetry offend you, and you speculate on the theory that it exhibits the limitations of the Indian mind. Yes, you say, it is just like these Baboos; they can learn and assimilate and reproduce, but they have not the innate strength, the prodigality of generative power, which characterises the great Gothic Englishman. What is the Taj to Durham, or Canterbury, or Winchester? But you are wrong. See the Taj: it will fascinate you so as to deprive you of all power of laudatory expression, and it will haunt you ever after till your dying day. It will float in the clear Tuscan air above the bell-tower of Giotto, and arise across the lagoon beside the Doge's palace and St. Mark's.

What is the reason of this charm? You drive towards the Taj from Agra, your gaze is fixed upon the deep red of the entrance gateway, you step beneath it and see at the end of a garden the vision you have longed for—a symmetrical building of dazzling pearly white. It seems unearthly and unreal, a mirage produced by some illusion of the eye. It is presented in a moment, unbidden, before the gaze satiated with crimson, and it will disappear as soon as the eye has recovered its natural functions. It is this shadowy unearthliness which distinguishes the Taj from all other buildings ; it rises like a phantom before you, as its image floated like a phantom before the brain of the artist who created it. From whatever point of view you look at it, it is the same—a snowy peak of symmetrical cloud, evoked from below the horizon of your ken by some magic of the Indian air, an illusion, but most real, a temple "never built and therefore built for ever."

Not that there is really anything unsubstantial about it. It is one of the most solid and best preserved buildings in the world. Every inch of it will bear inspection. The white marble is as dazzling, the richly encrusted ornaments as full of colour, as on the day when it was completed. I need not describe at length what every one knows. This marvellous erection, which dominates by the wonder of its entirety, fascinates also by the beauty of its details, and by the distinction of the thought which gave it birth. The ornaments, undoubtedly Italian in workmanship and design, although carried out by Indians, are always in perfect taste, and never more so than when they approach the tomb of the good wife and woman in whose honour it is erected. Let the traveller, when he has recovered from the first shock of surprise, satisfy himself of the solidity of the building which has caused it by wandering over every part, then let him examine every flower and sprig of the elaborate ornamentation, let the lessons of the pious inscriptions sink into his mind, then let him burn some fragrant incense before the tomb, and, as a last orison, let some rich voice utter some few sounds of praise. The music redoubled by each encircling chapel, and caught up into unity by the embracing dome, will sound in rich organ tones, surpassed by few earthly instruments, in praise of her whom the temple honours, and of Him who gave her to the world.

Besides a terrace overlooking the Jumna, a minaret at each corner commanding an interesting view, and a spacious marble courtyard, the Taj has before it a lovely garden, rich in roses and in strange trees, over which the flying-foxes glide noiselessly in the dusk. Always admired, it was at one time treated with the contempt which is bred by familiarity. Dances were held upon the marble platform, the buildings of the Taj were used as cloak-rooms, and it is said that the band penetrated even into the shrine itself. Similarly the garden was a favourite place for picnics. All this is now forbidden, mainly by the influence of the Viceroy, and the shrine is once more a sanctuary.

My Brahmin friend was indignant at the suggestion that the Taj owed anything to foreign workmen. But facts are against him. It is believed that the Florentine, who produced the design, if not of the Taj, at least of its ornaments, died early, and that his work was carried out by one Austin, of Bordeaux, who settled in India and has left descendants. We were told that one of these still survives, and that he has in his possession the original plans of the Taj, which have been of use in carrying out restorations. My first view of the Taj was through the red gateway, my last was from the railway as I left. It is the incomparable building of the world, and any praise which is given to any other building must always leave the Taj supreme.

Sikri

XIII

SIKRI

WITHOUT derogating from the supremacy of the Taj, some Anglo-Indians will tell you that the sight best worth seeing in their country is Futehpur-Sikri, an old town twenty-three miles distant from Agra. I should be disposed to agree with them ; certainly none of my experiences in India left so deep an impression on my mind. The title is a misnomer : the town you go to visit is Sikri ; Futehpur is merely the modern village which nestles under the hill on which Sikri stands. You will be told that it is the Pompeii of India.

Nothing can be more misleading. Certainly the hillside is covered with the ruins of former edifices, and much of the wall is no longer standing ; indeed, large tracts of it have ceased to exist in quite recent years. Also the Elephant Gate is not in the best state of preservation, and other gates have perished or were never built. But what you go to see is a palace, which might be inhabited to-morrow, some part of which, indeed, is inhabited, and a series of religious buildings which are maintained with loving care, and which will stand till the crack of doom.

The charm of Sikri lies in the fact that, whereas it is a magnificent palace, complete in every particular according to Oriental ideas, with sleeping-rooms and halls for public consultation, for repose and pleasure, with zenanas for the women, yet it has a spiritual origin, and the buildings in which these spiritual aspirations are enshrined are the most magnificent of the whole. So at King's College, Cambridge, the chapel, the founder's first care, is at once the germ and the crown of the rest of the buildings.

The Emperor Akbar, being blessed with daughters, greatly desired to have a son, and in his difficulty he consulted a holy man who dwelt at Sikri. The saint promised that he should have an heir, and when the promise was fulfilled Akbar determined to fix his residence upon the sacred spot. On a hill commanding plenty of fresh air and a glorious view, he built a palace, which was afterwards expanded into a town. He then determined to fortify it, but the saint objected that, if crowds of people came to live there, his devotions would be interrupted. Akbar, in the wayward manner of Oriental potentates, soon left this residence, it is said because the supply of good water was deficient; but the saint always lived there, and when he died he was buried with great pomp, and a majestic mosque was raised in his honour.

On arriving at Sikri you are received in a dâk bungalow, where you are indifferently entertained at a large price. This building is constructed, like the rest of Akbar's palace, of red stone, and was the public record office. It is a slur upon the English authorities at Agra that this fine specimen of architecture should be used for base purposes, and it is to be hoped that an hotel may soon be erected which will supply not only food, but beds for even the most distinguished travellers, who are now most improperly lodged in some of the most interesting rooms in the palace.

A large platform crowns the summit of the hill, and this is occupied by Akbar's bedroom, his hall of audience, and several other buildings. The needs of an Indian climate are very different from those of Europe, especially in a summer residence. No doors, windows, or fireplaces are necessary; a few hangings give everything that is required. There are two houses in the precincts, one of which is attributed to the Prime Minister of Akbar, and to his daughter who afterwards became the emperor's mistress. Her bedroom is a gem of art, with a dainty balcony and a spacious terrace. But it is difficult to defend its use as an Indian bathroom for the use of the commissioner and his friends. Such a profanation should not be allowed; it is offensive to an Englishman, and must be doubly so to natives.

As I am not writing a guide-book, I need not describe the buildings of Sikri in detail. Most striking is the Elephant Gateway, so called from the two large beasts which guard it, whose heads were cut off by the fanatic Aurungzebe, and the Elephant Tower, just opposite, looking like a tipsy-cake, in which the place of the almonds has been taken by elephants' tusks. A separate division of the palace is formed by the apartments of the women, constructed in Hindu architecture of a less refined type. Beyond this is a spacious court of dazzling marble. On one side is the tomb of the saint, incrusted with mother-of-pearl and precious stones, covered with costly hangings. You enter it with bare feet. The roof is supported by marble beams, carved in a strange shape. This same design is found in the stone-cutters' mosque, of which we shall speak presently. We walk round the tomb of the saint, without our shoes, full of the religion of the place. At the farther end of the square towers the huge mosque. An Indian mosque is not like a church; a wall with a space in front for worshippers to kneel in is all that is required, and, if more room is needed, it can be found in the court outside. Behind the mosque is the house where the saint lived, the modest tomb in which his bones were laid until they were removed to their present sumptuous abode, and the so-called mosque of the stone-cutters, the offering of the masons to the sanctity of the saint whom they commemorated. Close by is a deep-lying tank of greenish water, into which naked men and boys plunge feet foremost from a perilous height.

Such is Sikri, very imperfectly described in the poor words that I have used. It took us six hours of continuous walking, under a blazing sun, to see the whole of these treasures. I, at least, was not tired, but I was glad of the refreshing tea with which the dâk bungalow supplied us. Before we rejoined our carriage, we paid a visit to the Hammam, the bath, under the hill, built by Akbar's doctor and still well preserved. We were accompanied by a black young bhisti, who seemed to revel in the sight of the palace dedicated to his favourite liquid. It is supposed that much of the peculiar ornamentation of the vaulting of the Taj was copied from this bath.

The drive home was delicious. The jackals chased each other in merry play through the neighbouring fields. The black buck trotted through the forest, and an encampment of British Tommies, in a mango tope, showed the day's kill slung up to the branches, recalling Robin Hood in the forest of Sherwood. The wild boar fled from the approach of our horses, and the fireflies danced in the thickets. As we neared the town the stars shone with Indian brilliancy, the splendour of Orion making up for the loss of the Southern Cross, and after our long day we were glad to profit by the hospitality of the Agra Club.

Aligarh

XIV

ALIGARH

ALIGARH has for many years been one of the names best known to me in India. It is indissolubly connected with the memory of Theodore Beck, and no one who once knew Theodore Beck can ever forget him. He came up to Cambridge with a great reputation for mathematics, having won, I think, an entrance scholarship. His character presented a singularly harmonious balance between emotion and intellect; his beautiful face and long hair always reminded me of the traditional portraits of the Messiah. He soon became dissatisfied with the Cambridge method of studying his favourite science—that is, of hastily getting up a number of subjects, so as to be able to present them for examination, but not to pursue them to a useful end. He therefore rebelled, and read mathematics in his own way, and in consequence reached a very low place in his college examinations.

The authorities were indignant, and wrote to his father, who, however, replied that he had always allowed his sons to take their own course in the development of their minds, and that he saw no reason to alter his practice in the present instance. Eventually Beck obtained only a second class in the Tripos, and was therefore debarred from entering for the second part, in which he might have distinguished himself. He therefore found himself, at the end of his academical career, with many brilliant friends, and a high reputation among them, but with no outward qualification for a post by which he might earn his living.

Beck had long been interested in Orientals and in their modes of thought and life, and just at this time Syed Ahmed came to England in search of a principal for the Mohammedan College which he was founding at Aligarh. Chance brought him across Beck, who applied himself with great zeal to find the person of whom Syed Ahmed was in search. All exertions proved in vain, when Syed Ahmed suddenly told Beck, to his great surprise, that he had been so favourably impressed with his qualities, during his intercourse with him, that he was convinced that no one was so fit to be head of the new college as himself.

Beck accepted with alacrity, and entered upon his duties with a single-minded zeal and devotion which could not be surpassed.

It was Theodore's habit at this time to write long letters to his mother, giving a minute account of all his experiences in his new life, relating all the difficulties which he met with, his successes and his failures, his triumphs and his mistakes, discussing with singular impartiality, in each case, whether he had been right or wrong in his judgments. These letters were copied into a book, and circulated amongst intimate friends. I was privileged to read them, and thus the early fortunes of Aligarh became very familiar to me. Beck did a great work, and left a name which will always live in the grateful mind of Indians. He killed himself by overtoil, and by refusal to take a holiday. He died at Simla, his last hours soothed by the tender care of Lady Curzon; and so his mortal life ended, but his spiritual life has only just begun, and will long continue to inspire the institution for which he lived and died, and many similar institutions which are certain to arise from it. He has a worthy successor in Theodore Morison, who was for some time his colleague.

Aligarh lies in the most visited part of India, between Agra and Delhi. Morison met me at the station, and took me to his house, which had been the home of Beck. It is the only house which I visited in India in which abundant signs of culture were apparent. The walls were covered with pictures, and the shelves were lined with books. I wonder whether any one in India, excepting Morison and the

Gaekwar of Baroda, possesses what may be called a library?

This absence of culture, however obvious and regrettable, is not to be wondered at. The civil servant is so much occupied with desk-work that he has no time or inclination for any recreation except sport. He leads an ambulatory existence, he may be removed at a moment's notice from one station to another, he has nothing about him which may be called a home. How is he to transport over the long stretches of Indian travel boxes of books and cases of pictures? The country swarms with the worst enemies of books. White ants eat up the bindings and devour the contents; fish insects, a horror of which I often heard, but which I never saw, are even more destructive. Let any one visit the great library at Calcutta, which the Viceroy is attempting to reorganise under Mr. Macfarlane in the Metcalfe Hall. A scurvier set of volumes was never presented to the human gaze; they look as if they had been wrecked in the Indian Ocean, and laboriously recovered by pearl-divers. Under these circumstances Anglo-Indians may be excused if they have few books or pictures; but those who possess them in spite of these difficulties should have a double share of honour.

The College of Aligarh covers a large space of ground, and has many buildings of a single story, as is common in India. The centre is occupied by a large hall, erected in memory of Sir John Strachey, which, when I was there, was being used for an examination. The students are very numerous, and seemed happy and contented, and much given to games. They all wore the long coat and the cap which distinguish Mohammedans from Hindus. They certainly looked older than English students, the boys of nineteen who were being examined appearing to me like young men of five-and-twenty, while beards and whiskers were very noticeable.

The results of Aligarh education are known to every Cambridge man. The founders of the college not only wished to place half the population of India in as good a position to receive instruction as the other half, but they thought that if the up-country Mohammedans, who are of a manlier type than the Bengalis, and who are lovers of the open air, could only be persuaded to adopt literary tastes and to train their minds, they might exercise a great influence over the future of their country. Whether this can be done still remains to be seen. I have no statistics before me, but I believe that the natives who have obtained places in the Civil Service are for the most part Hindus. The importance of the work done at Aligarh cannot be overrated, and the influence of a colony of cultivated English men and women upon those who surround them, to whatever nationality they belong, is a precious possession for our great dependency.

My arrangements only allowed me twenty-four hours in this interesting place. As I drove to the station, I was able to inspect the Theodore Beck wall, an erection well known to his friends, as it is built in sections, each of which is inscribed with the name of the person who paid for it. I found also at the station the newspapers announcing the fact that I had been appointed the first Minister of Education under Lord Curzon, and for forty-eight hours I enjoyed the amusement of being the innocent object of the gossip of a continent. As I was acquainted with the Viceroy's plans, I knew the news to be false, and that nothing more was in contemplation than the establishment of a General Director of Education, who should bring the work of the provincial directors into harmony. I knew also that the post had been offered to Mr. Orange, of the Education Office, and had been accepted by him. But some day or other a Minister of Education will have to be appointed, as no one with less authority than a member of the Viceroy's Council will be able to weld into a consistent whole the confused chaos of Indian education, and to give educational questions their due importance by the side of the other interests which occupy the attention of the rulers of our Indian Empire.

Delhi

XV

DELHI

MY Brahmin friend, who had been my guide through Benares and Agra, was not able to accompany me to Delhi, from an attack of illness; and I should have been like a pelican in the wilderness, if his place had not been supplied by a Mohammedan friend, also a graduate of Cambridge, who took possession of me when I arrived, and did not relax his kindly care until he had seen me safely installed in the train for Baroda. Delhi, or, as it ought to be called, Dehli, is the real capital of India—that is, it is the capital of the dynasty which ruled India for many generations with majesty and power, and made her name respected throughout Europe and the world. The extinction of the line of the Mogul Emperors gave the best guarantee for the permanence of the British Raj, as it removed all competitors who could claim the throne with any show of right.

At the same time Delhi, the city, can hardly be called a capital; indeed, its proper name is Shahjahanabad, the city of Shah Jahan. The country for miles round Delhi is covered with the remains of cities, more or less conspicuous, which have been the capitals of Mogul sovereigns at different times. Akbar, as we have seen, had his capital at Agra, and was nearly placing it at Sikri. When the Viceroy held his great Durbar at Delhi on January 1st, 1903, he called into existence a new city of twenty thousand inhabitants, furnished with roads, tramways, a complete system of drainage and water supply, electric light, and other appliances of civilisation. It lasted only for a few weeks, but it was an exact counterpart to the other centres of power, which in that wide plain have enjoyed an ephemeral existence. The reason why the fort of Delhi has been regarded for so long as the central palace of India is not so much because the Mogul Emperors fixed their seat there for two centuries, as that, having once chosen it as their habitation, they were not strong enough to found another.

The central attraction of Delhi is, of course, the fort, now a place of British arms, but formerly a fortified palace. It contains the building which, next to the

Taj, impresses its image on the traveller's mind more than anything else in India—I mean the private hall of audience, the Dewan-i-Khas. Like other Indian buildings, no description can portray it, no photograph give an idea of it, no painting represent it. Let me copy what the guide-book says of it: "Proceeding towards the left, the Hall of Special Audience, the House of Lords, is reached; a smaller hall, in echelon to the first, raised on a small marble estrade, about four feet high, with a small but chastely carved balustrade of perforated marble on the front side. The columns of this, the finest hall of its kind in India, are inlaid below with precious stones in floral designs, the upper section, as well as the ceiling and cornice, being very tastefully gilt."

What idea can these words give to

the reader of this wonderful creation, dignified as a shrine, jewelled like a brooch, dazzling as a pearl, symmetrical as a flower? The white and gold of the roof and the upper story are in perfect taste, and produce quite a new impression, notwithstanding the hackneyed recurrence of these tints in modern decoration. The artist must have conceived the effect of these decussating arches, of the play of delicate colours under an Indian sun, before he could have given orders for the work. The Dewan-i-Khas remains a standard and a touchstone, by which all the great palaces of the world may be tried and estimated.

A returning Indian, after reading all that Ruskin has to say about the Doge's Palace at Venice, will decide that it is not comparable to the Dewan-i-Khas at Delhi. The builder must have been conscious of the worth of his ideal, for has he not written on the walls the famous inscription, paralleled, indeed, elsewhere, but nowhere so complete and obvious, "Agar furduse baru-i-zamin ast, hamin ast, hamin ast, hamin ast," which loses something in Moore's translation, "If there be an elysium on earth, it is this, it is this, it is this"? This hall also contained the peacock throne, which, if it was designed by Austin of Bordeaux, must have been much more beautiful than "the four-post bed with two peacocks and a parrot perched upon the testers," of which the guide-books tell us.

It is needless to speak of the other buildings of the palace, so many of which were destroyed in the Mutiny, or have since been ruined by British restorations, or converted to the base uses of officers' quarters. The bathrooms, which must originally have surpassed the Alhambra in loveliness, whose ceilings offer tantalising traces of exquisite ornamentation, have been carefully white or blue washed by the P.W.D.

The Tommy who showed us round explained that this had been done for sake of decency. The British soldiers, entering the palace after the suppression of the Mutiny, found the decoration of these vaultings quite too shocking. The pictures were immediately covered up, so that they might not corrupt the soldiers' morals, nor offend their taste; and they could never, he said, be uncovered so long as the British were masters of Delhi. We did not tell him, what we remarked to each other, that as the Mussulman is strictly forbidden to represent the human or, indeed, any animal form, any such designs must have been confined to the loves of the plants, which might be considered as innocuous even to the most perverted imagination.

Dear Tommy! you were so good, so well-informed, so conscientious, so anxious to give every explanation, and, withal, so philistine and so stupid, that I was quite charmed with you, and so was my native companion. I was proud to be your fellow-countryman. When you showed me the balances in the Hall of Justice, and said that the judges had to pray before them when about to pronounce their dooms, I suggested that the next time you were condemned to a fortnight's C.B., you should ask your commanding officer whether he had duly offered that prayer. But you will never be condemned; you will leave your regiment with a stainless character.

Just outside the fort of Delhi stands the Jamna Musjid, the great mosque, another creation of Shah Jahan. It is remarkable that the great works of this mighty builder were constructed when our own country was in the throes of a civil war and a political revolution; when Germany was being devastated by the Thirty Years' War; when France was in disorder, and Italy unquiet. Can these events have caused an emigration of foreign workmen to India? The great features of the mosque are its enormous size and its dignified magnificence.

We visited it on Friday, which is the Mohammedan Sunday, and found the large court full of worshippers. We took off our shoes, and ascended the summit of the highest tower, which commands a splendid view. While we were there a dead body was brought in, carried on a bamboo bier, and covered with a sheet of unsullied muslin. The bearers brought the corpse to the edge of the large washing-tank which occupies the centre of the court. The worshippers thronged round it, a short service was held, and the body was carried off by the left-hand porch. My Mohammedan friend told me that it would be buried without any further ceremony.

The treatment of the Mohammedan dead appeared to me even more simple than that of the Hindoos. There was no outward sign of mourning or lamentation, "nothing was here for tears, nothing to wail," at the same time there was nothing to show indifference to the loss, no doubt as to a future state. I was fortunate to have seen the great mosque under such favourable circumstances. As my companion and myself, believer and unbeliever, walked side by side, no disrespect was offered to me. We looked with sympathy at the prostrate worshippers, and at the holy saint who had consecrated his life to prayer and fasting, and who was surrounded by a crowd of devotees. My friend assured me that he was a convinced Mohammedan, and that the only difference between us was that he placed Mahomet by the side of Christ. He did not anticipate any great conversion of the Mussulmans to Christianity, but he hoped that the votaries of the two religions might some day come to understand each other.

Old Delhi

XVI

OLD DELHI

HE who would visit ancient Delhi must drive out eleven miles from the present city, when he will find himself at the fort of Lalkot, the date of which is nearly coeval with the Norman Conquest. Although the name of Delhi is now indissolubly connected with the Mogul Emperors, a large Hindu city existed under that appellation, which ceased to be a royal residence less than a hundred years after the birth of Christ. In the middle of the eighth century it was rebuilt by the Rajputs, and it was not finally conquered by the Mussulmans until the last years of the twelfth century.

The Mohammedan invaders naturally wished to commemorate their triumphs by the erection of a mosque, and for this purpose they used already existing Hindu pillars, having obliterated any features which were offensive to them. The mosque, if finished, would have been of enormous size, but the feature of it which chiefly attracts the traveller is the Kutab Minar, the lofty minaret which forms so conspicuous an object from the walls of Delhi, and which is at once fastened upon as a goal of pilgrimage. It dates from the first thirty years of the thirteenth century, and is, therefore, coeval with the double church at Assisi, which is supposed to be the earliest Gothic building erected in Italy, and is nearly contemporary with the Cathedral of Siena.

It is, probably, the most impressive minaret in the world ; it rises like the flower of a mighty aloe-tree to the height of 240 feet, becoming more slender as it ascends. It is fluted and divided into five stories, each of which has its own balcony. The view from the top extends to the walls of Delhi and over the plain, which is strewed with the ruins of the successive cities which have been built upon the site.

Close by this wonderful minaret stands another curious memorial of a very peculiar character. It is a simple iron pillar. In London it would be the remains of a dilapidated lamp-post, in Cambridge one of the ventilating shafts of our new system of drainage ; at Lalkot it is an object of worship. That this iron pillar should have been set up in the midst of so much magnificence as if it were of gold or of some precious marble has an indescribable effect upon the imagination. It is only twenty-two feet high, and was made after the fashion of the early guns, by welding together successive cylinders of metal. Its surface is smooth and uniform, in fact its dignity resides in its general insignificance. A Sanskrit inscription, cut upon one of its sides, is held to assign it to the epoch of Constantine the Great, but by whom it was erected or why no one knows, except that we may conclude that it was a personal memorial. Ladies generally despise it, but, take it all in all, it is one of the most interesting monuments which I saw in India.

I must confess that the other remains of Ancient Delhi have left on my mind rather a vague impression. I have a confused recollection of lofty walls; of ruined mosques; of tombs of holy men and kings, covered with flowers or with precious tapestries, to be approached with reverence by the pious; of tanks of green water into which men and boys plunged or were ready to plunge for annas; of a comfortable dâk bungalow, and of Sir Thomas Metcalfe's billiard-room. Some few images stand up prominently in the waste of ideas, as the monuments which I am describing rose from the waste of ideals.

One of these is the village of Nizam-ud-din, which contains several important monuments. There is the "hall of sixty-four pillars," supporting twenty-five domes, and the tomb of Akbar's foster-brother. There is the tomb of the great Shah Nizam-ud-din himself, who was a contemporary of the poet Dante. It is not devoid of magnificence, and is an object of great devotion. The guide-book asserts, on the authority of General Sleeman, that Nizam-ud-din was the founder of Thuggism. Sleeman formed his opinion from the fact that the Thugs worshipped at his tomb with especial reverence. I was earnestly requested by the attendant priests to give the most uncompromising denial to this monstrous calumny. The Thugs, they tell me, are very pious people, who worship all who deserve worship. They do not pray at the tomb of Nizam-ud-din more than they pray at the tomb of any other recognised saint, and if Nizam-ud-din were aware of their practices, he would regard them with unmitigated horror.

More interesting to me, I confess, was the tomb of the poet Khusru, whose verses I have never read, and shall never read. He lived at the court of Toghlak Shah, like Dante at the court of Can Grande, and, as Sleeman says, " moved about where he pleased through the palace of the emperor, and sang extempore songs to his lyre, while the greatest and fairest watched his lips to catch the expressions as they came warm from his soul." Orientals certainly have their own way of recognising and rewarding literary genius.

More conspicuous is the tomb of Humayun, about a mile from the fort of Delhi. It was built by Akbar to the memory of his father, and is said to have occupied the labour of two hundred masons for sixteen years. It contains eighteen tombs, six of which commemorate Mogul Emperors, and the rest of them their generals and counsellors. The tomb of Humayun is a forerunner of the Taj, not in the matchless beauty of its material or its ornament, for it is chiefly of red stone, and is plain in design. But its most haunting memory is that it was the last refuge of the miserable princes of the Royal House of Delhi, who were dragged from it to be killed. In a little recess off the great hall were huddled these cowering imbeciles, guilty of little but their rank, surrounded by a throng of faithful but cowed retainers, betrayed by one of their own blood. Hodson and Macdowell broke through the marble screen to seize them. Their lives were promised them, but the promise could not be kept.

As we drive back to Delhi, we pass the citadel and fort of Indraput, the capital of Sher Shah and Humayun, once, we are told, twice as large as Shahjahanabad, the modern Delhi. Here also is the scene of Humayun's death. Rising too suddenly at the call of prayer, he fell down a flight of steep stairs, and lay stunned at the bottom. He walked to his palace, but died of internal injuries.

Delhi is the Rome of India, but whilst India is English it can never be its capital. Calcutta has that position, and must maintain it. The capital of our commercial Empire must be situated, like London, on a great river, with easy access to the sea. But Delhi, like Rome, will always exercise a strong influence over the minds of all the races which inhabit the peninsula. It was the place where Queen Victoria was proclaimed Empress, it is the place where her son was proclaimed Emperor; and from its central position, and the memories by which it is consecrated, it will always remain the place of assembly for the tribes of India, when they go up united for any great civil or religious purpose.

Baroda

XVII

BARODA

SOME years ago, when I was staying at the Maloia, in the Engadine, the Gaekwar of Baroda, who had just arrived, sent to ask if I would receive him in my room. I was somewhat agitated at the idea of entertaining a reigning prince in an hotel bedroom, but I made the best arrangements that I could, and we talked over many things for a long time. Our conversation was principally concerned with the education of Indians at English universities. Before we parted I promised His Highness that, if ever I visited India,

I would pay him a visit, and as Baroda lay on the road between Delhi and Bombay, it was easy for me to fulfil my engagement. No one has seen India properly who has not visited a Native State; it is better indeed, if he can, to visit several of them. They retain much of the ancient appearance, and many of the old customs which have perished under the British Raj. If well administered they are interesting, if badly administered they are picturesque. They form a very important part of our system of government. Their existence is an earnest that we hold India as the trustees of the Indian people. They are useful, also, as a comparison with our own methods of administration. So long as the Rajahs are loyal, they are a great support to the throne. Their wealth forms a reservoir which, like that of the City companies, can be tapped for extraordinary purposes. No Viceroy would now meddle with the independence of the Native States. It is generally admitted that the annexation of Oude, and the fear lest it might be followed by similar acts, were among the principal causes of the Mutiny. To educate native princes, to make them English without ceasing to be Indian, to inspire them with the desire and the capacity for good government without severing them from their subjects, and making them merely the vassals of the court and the companions of English nobility, is a difficult problem. It is one, however, which the present Viceroy has set himself to solve, and in proportion as he succeeds so will the fortunes of the Native States be prosperous.

The Gaekwar of Baroda is a very remarkable man. He is enlightened and hard-working, his whole heart is given to the improvement of his people. It has been objected that he spends too much of his money on palaces, and of his time in Europe. But neither of these charges was supported by what I saw in my visit. It is true that he has constructed, at the cost, perhaps, of half a million, a large palace outside the town. But his ancestors lived in a wooden house in the midst of the city, a place quite out of harmony with modern conditions. The palace at Baroda is not too large for the requirements of a court in which the women live in purdah, nor is it better furnished than many English country houses. It did not cost nearly as much as Eaton Hall, which the Duke of Westminster built for the delectation of travelling Americans.

The Gaekwar's tours in Europe have

always been conducted for the benefit of his countrymen. In these journeys he has collected a fund of knowledge and experience which has enabled him to govern his estates in accordance with modern principles, and the Museum of Baroda shows with what judgment the money which he has spent in Europe has been laid out. It is filled with objects collected from the civilised world, of literary, artistic, and scientific interest, best calculated to stimulate the curiosity and to improve the education of his subjects. It was a touching sight to watch the crowds of natives, men, women, and children, as they thronged the galleries, delighted and instructed by the treasures which their sovereign had collected for them.

Baroda offers to the traveller the spectacle of a thoroughly well governed Native

State. It has of late years been sorely tried by famine, but the people seem happy and contented. Everywhere there are broad roads, well watered, pleasant groves, picturesque houses, the abode either of ministers or of members of the royal family. The Maharajah does everything for the comfort and amusement of his guests. They are met at the station by royal carriages, and conducted to a spacious guest-house, as it would be impossible for them to be lodged in the palace of the Gaekwar. They may stay as long as they please, and they are shown all the sights of the city.

There is a noble college, with ample, airy class-rooms, and competent English teachers; there is a hospital conducted on the best principles of modern science; there is a gaol in which the prisoners are, if anything, too well off, as the climate of India does not lend itself to solitary confinement. The palace of the Maharajah possesses an extensive library, chiefly of English books, which is open to every one. Europe has not a useful lesson which the Gaekwar has not done his best to learn, and to convey in fitting measure to his countrymen.

I was fortunate enough to have as my guide and companion an old Cambridge pupil, a Brahmin of high rank, the most brilliant Greek scholar whom I ever examined for an entrance scholarship. He obtained a place in the Indian Civil Service, but was rejected for his riding, and the Gaekwar has wisely attached him to his service. He is now engaged in important literary work, and he may some day be Minister of Education. We established a kind of blood-brotherhood between us by riding together on an elephant, an experience which neither of us had undergone before. The beast seemed to tower aloft, higher than any elephant I had ever seen. He knelt down, and we crawled to our seats on either side of him. It was a terrible moment when the animal rose to his legs, and we had to contemplate the possibility of slowly sliding to the ground down that long stretch of dark grey skin. This difficulty past, we rode slowly through the crowded streets, attracting, to my disappointment, very little attention. Elephants, strange as they were to me, are mere drugs in Baroda, but we were both relieved when we reached the palace where we were to see the jewels. The elephant awaited our return, but we preferred the carriage. "Do men ever hunt twice?"

Lord Chesterfield is reported to have said. Neither my friend nor myself had any desire to mount an elephant a second time.

We saw some strange sights in the native town. A snake-charmer and conjurer was surrounded by a large crowd at the corner of a street. We stopped the carriage to look at him. For our special delectation he ripped up his boy attendant's stomach, and stowed away the body in a basket, from which the lad soon afterwards emerged, alive and smiling. I had only two opportunities of seeing Indian conjuring, but on neither occasion did it appear to me at all remarkable, except as regarded sleight of hand. The growth of the mango-tree, the murder of the boy, the snake-charming, and some of the other tricks were interesting and picturesque to watch, but could not appear supernatural to the most indifferent observer.

I also had the good fortune to witness a marriage procession. During the latter half of the month of February, the money-lending caste seemed to be marrying in profusion, and we had seen signs of it at Futehpur and at Delhi. The procession was a long one, accompanied by bands of music. The bridegroom, a child of ten, was covered from head to foot with cloth of gold and flowers, and seemed to be much amused as he rode upon his quiet steed. Before him rode on horseback numerous groomsmen, all younger than himself, with richly embroidered robes and caps. Little girls accompanied the procession, carried in litters, with red marks on their foreheads, showing that they were already wives. The bridegroom was on his way to the bride's house, to see her for the first time; he would see her and then depart, and they would not keep house together till some years had passed. Horses are necessary accompaniments of a Hindu marriage. If the real animals cannot be provided, paper models are substituted, which are cunningly made and are very cheap.

We were also shown some parrots, carefully trained to climb ladders and to fire off guns, and some rams who butted at each other with a violence which seemed likely to smash their skulls. We visited the beautiful public gardens, laid out in exquisite taste, where an orchestra discourses both Indian and European music, under the baton of a conductor who has been trained at Leipzig. This is also highly appreciated by the natives.

At last, all too soon, came the time

for departure. My friend accompanied me to the crowded train, where I had with some difficulty secured a lower berth. I was to wake up next morning in Bombay, the last stage of my travel.

Elephanta

XVIII

ELEPHANTA

MY companion at Government House, Bombay, Monsignore of the Roman Church and a protonotary apostolic, was anxious to visit the caves of Elephanta, and I was of the same mind. The Governor kindly ordered his steam launch to be got ready, and we left the Apollo Bunder in the afternoon, with the design of returning before dinner. The launch was small, and the wind was contrary as well as cold, and when we got out into the open bay the waves began to rise and splashed into the boat. I had implicit confidence in the seaworthiness of the launch, and the experience of the crew; but I am not sure that my feelings were shared by my companion. However, after a somewhat intricate voyage, we reached the island on which the caves are situated. The landing was not altogether easy. We had to step into a small boat and were rowed to a rickety pier, after which our path lay partly over crazy woodwork, and partly over lumps of concrete, divided by deep fissures. However, we reached our goal in safety.

The path from the landing-place to the caves has been laid down in the form of a brick causeway by some pious Hindu, so that it presents no difficulty, even to the most indifferent walker. But in India no one is expected to walk at all, and therefore sedan-chairs are provided, with men to carry them. It seemed to me a needless luxury to entrust my weight to these conveyances, and to be carried by four men up a very gradual ascent; so I stepped out boldly towards the summit. But as soon as I set out to return I discovered my mistake. I had become heated even in that short ascent, and I had to face a return in a small boat with a cold wind, and, however much I wrapped myself up, I was doomed to catch a chill. Such, indeed, was the case, and I committed my first act of imprudence on the last day which I spent in India.

The island is called Gharapuri by the Hindus, and Elephanta is a name given by the Portuguese. The great cave, which alone attracts the ordinary traveller, is two hundred and fifty feet above the level of the sea. It is dedicated to the worship of Shiva, and is frequented mainly by the Banias, or money-lending caste, who seek here not so much forgiveness for any deceitful action of which they may have been guilty, as assistance in any enterprise which they are about to undertake. "Da mihi fallere" is a prayer which has reached us from pagan times.

I am not sufficiently well acquainted with the Hindu mythology to give any useful account of the carved images to be found in the caves, but there is no doubt that worship held in these cavernous temples, especially at night, when the monstrous forms would be lit up by torches, would be impressive to the imagination. The visitor, on entering, is met by a huge figure of Brahma, the creator, supported by Vishnu, the preserver, on the right, and by Shiva, the destroyer, on the left. This is the Trimurti, the three-faced figure, the

Hindu Trinity. Brahma bears in his hand a pomegranate, Vishnu a lotus flower, and Shiva a cobra, emblems of their respective attributes. The triple deity is attended by two doorkeepers and two dwarfs.

The most sacred room in the building contains the usual Hindu emblem of the generative power of nature. When the temple was in regular use, the four doors which enclose this shrine were only opened once a year, at the great Shiva festival, held just before the new moon which occurs in the month of February, and even now it is believed by the Banian ladies not to have lost its efficacy. The figures are supposed to have been carved in the sixth century before the Christian era, and are therefore coeval with the earliest remains of Greek sculpture. They have little beauty to recommend them, although the guide is careful to tell us that one of the heads bears a striking resemblance to our late revered Queen. Those who worshipped them must have regarded the divinity as a power rather to be feared and propitiated than to be loved and imitated. Shiva is represented in various aspects: here he is being married, there he is sacrificing a child, in one place he is intoxicated and is playing a tune with one of his eight arms, in another he is mourning for the loss of his wife. Then there are more Lingam shrines, one with a stone bull watching the emblem, as we find it at Benares; and a bathroom fed by water which is supposed to be conveyed in some mysterious manner from the Ganges.

I must confess that my visit was a hurried one. I had my eye on the tossing launch and the white horses of the bay, and I thought of my suffering companion. As darkness was coming on we hastened rapidly down the causeway, traversed the concrete mole, with its yawning chasms, which recalled the bridge of Rasselas, entered the little boat and reached the launch in safety. But the unexpected happened: the wind sank with the sinking sun, the little steamer made good way upon an even keel, we were able to enjoy our hospitable tea, and before we expected it we were again at the Apollo Bunder, found the Governor's carriage waiting for us, and drove to Malabar Hill under the brightness of Indian stars.

It is said that men built temples in caves not so much from piety as from economy, as you have no floor or roof to provide, and your walls are ready for the sculptor's chisel. However this may be, I think that Elephanta would be more impressive upon the stage than in reality. When I next see the "Magic Flute," or read of the Eleusinian Mysteries, I shall remember that I have visited a place where scenes may have been enacted which would have appalled the stoutest heart, and he who had passed through them might well believe that he was steeled against mere earthly troubles, and could climb with a confident spirit the steep and difficult path which leads to the richest guerdon of the unseen.

The Voyage Home

XIX

THE VOYAGE HOME

MY visit to India was at an end. As I had come out by the Messageries Maritimes and the Gulf of Lyons, I determined to return by the Austrian Lloyd and the Adriatic—a course which is made easy by the companies issuing circular tickets, which are available by either route. The good ship *Imperatrix* was to sail at noon on March 1st, 1902, and having been declared free from plague, and having taken leave, to my abundant sorrow, of my beloved bearer Antony, of whom I cannot speak too highly, I went on board and arranged my cabin, which was to be my home for the next three weeks.

We were a singularly happy company, mainly English, of different vocations and occupations. There was a judge of the High Court, and a resident from a Native State, each accompanied by their families, a retired colonel gazing with regretful eyes at the country he was leaving, two gallant English officers of whom any country might be proud, cheerful, intelligent, manly, and modest, forming a happy and united family, into which no disposition, however contentious, could introduce discord.

The second class was occupied almost entirely by missionaries, who contributed largely to the gaiety and profit of the voyage. They held services on Sunday, and conducted high jinks on other nights with a spirit and vigour of which our dignity allowed us to partake, although it would not suffer us to imitate. The officers of the ship were indefatigable in their duties; they seemed to be continually taking observations, four of them at once, and marking our place upon the chart, and in fine weather we were freely admitted to the chart-room, to see what progress we had made.

The Indian Ocean was singularly kind to us, the weather was warm with a refreshing breeze, and for twenty-four hours the sea wore that oily appearance which is only met with in the tropics. There was little animal life; one passenger, I believe, found a flying-fish in his cabin, a few porpoises played around us, and we were accompanied by occasional gulls. One day the sea-serpent appeared in the offing, but those armed with the best glasses declared it to be a whale. When we arrived at Aden, on the seventh day, we agreed that we had passed a perfect time.

At Aden we visited the famous tanks, wnich were now devoid of water, we bought ostrich-feathers and other doubtful products of Arabia, and at night entered the Red Sea. Here we had a splendid view of the Southern Cross, which I had not seen on the outward journey. One had to get up in the middle of the night to look at it, but it was well worth the exertion. It is the fashion to depreciate this constellation, but, whether from associations or from intrinsic merit, it impressed me deeply. These four stars, only seen, as Dante tells us, by our first parents in Eden, forming a Latin cross, which was when we saw it placed in the right position, was a spectacle from which it was difficult to withdraw one's gaze. And not the least important part of the pageant were the two pointers, the alpha and beta Centauri, the first of them the brightest star in the sky, who solemnly marked it with their astral fingers. Night after night I rose to gaze at the cross, till nothing remained of it except the pointers, indicating where it had sunk.

Our first day in the Red Sea was considered to be rough, a change due as much to the currents as to the wind; and, when the sea became smooth again, the weather was very hot. The thermometer reached 90° Fahr., whereas at no time in India had it exceeded 80°, and old travellers declared their intention of sleeping on deck. I preferred my roomy cabin, even with the port closed, and I believe that I had the best of it. On the twelfth day from Bombay we reached Suez, but did not land. A strong wind was blowing, and it was bitterly cold. Great preparations had been made by kodakers for taking photographs in the Canal, but our whole passage was marred by a violent sand-storm, a blizzard of the desert, cold and penetrating, making the eyes sore and the temper ruffled. Nothing however, could impair the harmony of our family and the gaiety of our officers. We landed at Port Said, which on going out had seemed to me a chosen example of the East, but which now appeared repulsively European. I longed once more for the tropics, the opulent sunshine, and the swarthy forms. Outside the sea looked very rough, and we shuddered at the sight of the sandy water.

We were not mistaken. It was very stormy in the night, and something, we were told, we had carried away. Crete appeared, barren and inhospitable, but it protected us from the strong north wind. In stormy weather we passed under the snows of Ida and the crags of Cerigotto and Cerigo, till rounding the Morea brought us a little respite. Sunday was a perfect day. Our excellent captain chose the smoothest passage for us, and every hour had its own delight. Zante was passed at sunrise, then came Ithaca and Cephalonia, with many inquiries after Penelope and Laertes, Telemachus and Eumaeus. Next followed Leucadia and Sappho's leap, Paxo and Antipaxo and Corfu. We could see the palace of the Austrian Empress, the bereaved mourner, the maniac's victim. We passed the Ambracian Gulf, with Actium and Nicopolis, where Byron mourned for Thyrza, and where a world was won and lost. The coast of Epirus and Albania offered many opportunities for the photographer, although we did not know that a rebellion was seething within those iron hills, and that the ships which we were taking might be carrying arms against the Turks.

The last day of our voyage brought us to the Dalmatian coast. We were signalled to Trieste from Lissa, the scene of the naval battle between the Austrians and the Italians in 1866. On Tuesday morning we arrived at Trieste, a smaller, less interesting, and less active Genoa. Glad as we were to reach the land, we were sorry that the voyage had come to an end, which was so full of pleasant memories, and had united us in a bond of friendship. For myself the dream was over, and I was waking up to stern realities. Even though

I have written these pages, I can scarcely believe that I have been in India. A vision seems to have opened and closed before me as I slept. The sutures of ordinary life are now joined again, and the Indian interlude has sunk into my subliminal consciousness, to arise ever and anon as a delusion too brilliant to be true.

Conclusion

XX

CONCLUSION

PUBLICISTS who have travelled in India and who moralise upon what they have seen are accustomed to observe that the two great obstacles to progress in that country are purdah and caste, and that until these are removed no improvement is possible. I am not myself of that opinion. Purdah, or the seclusion of women, is of course repugnant to our feelings and contrary to our habits, but I have sometimes wished that we had just a little of it in our own country, and that the spirit which produces it in India was not in danger of becoming extinct amongst ourselves. My native friends assured me that purdah is not, strictly, a Hindoo practice, but that it was introduced by the Mohammedan conquerors, who maintained it for obvious reasons, and was made fashionable by them. It certainly does not exist amongst the lower classes of the Hindu women, who are often seen uncovered in the streets.

But since it has made its way into the habits and the social feelings of the better class of Hindu women, any attempt to remove it would meet with their strong opposition. It is to their minds a mark of delicacy and refinement, and you might as well expect a marchioness to take her pot of beer at the bar of a public-house, as a high-born Hindu lady to expose herself to the public gaze. My Brahmin friend at Ghazipur was bringing up his wife to mix in society as an English lady would; but it was in vain that I asked to be allowed to call upon his mother, who would have been shocked at such a violation of the laws of purdah. It is probable that in time purdah will gradually disappear; but so long as women are regarded as refining influences in the world, so long as men have to learn what is becoming from the other sex, so long, I hope, will the veil of seclusion be only gradually lifted from the Indian Zenana. Purdah does not imply that women are not the companions of their husbands, or that they do not form the character of their sons; it means that they seek their strength in seclusion, and that they feel that seclusion to be the source and the safeguard of their best virtues.

Caste is far more defensible; indeed, in many respects it coincides with the highest social ideals which are held out to us by leaders of thought. Does not Ruskin preach that a man should choose his occupation when young, should follow it with zeal for its own sake, should not desire to change it, but should try to do his duty in it as well as possible and be contented with it till he dies? What is this but caste? I do not know how many castes there are in India, but as a fact all important occupations are organised in this manner. For my own part I trust that if I am ever born again, in India, I may become a bhisti, or water-carrier. I am told that they are most excellent people. Does not Mr. Kipling's Gunga Din testify to the fact that their name is a title of honour? Certainly their occupation is most beneficent. With their mussack or goatskin on their back, they are always either watering the roads, or giving drink to animals, or refreshing the weary traveller. But if to be a bhisti is good, what must it be to be born a bhisti, to feel from your earliest years that your profession is chosen for you, and that all you have to do is to be contented with it, to do it as well as you can, and not to suffer that those who went before you should have done it better?

But if caste does away with many of the discontents and unhappinesses of life, it is also a powerful social engine for moral behaviour. The rules of caste are very strict, and the caste council, which sees that they are properly observed, is inexorable. Neither rank nor wealth can escape from its authority. Any contravention of the written or unwritten rules of caste will secure a punishment which is all the more severe from being of a social character. Thus caste, while it keeps a man contented and finds him occupation, also jealously guards his conduct. It is of course incompatible with competition, with the struggle in life for place and power, and for the survival of the fittest. It may be well that caste should be slowly weakened in order that India may become a progressive country. But there is much to be said for it. It is the solid foundation of social order and morality, and any interference with it would produce terrible results. My visit to India persuaded me to tolerate purdah, and to have an admiration for caste, and I should be sorry to hear that either of them had been overthrown.

No one who has applied himself to the study of politics will be of opinion that parliamentary government, or even self-government, is applicable to all kinds of people in all conditions and in all times, and few persons who have been in India will desire to see the autocratic system of government which prevails there materially altered. It is difficult to imagine a machinery by which the government of India might be transferred, even partially, to the hands of the Indian people. If that is impossible, and the Congress has not discovered a manner in which it might be introduced, we are thrown back upon the personal government of the Viceroy, advised by his Council and controlled by the India Office. If personal government is to exist at all, it must be strong, or its weakness will result in misery to the governed. I cannot imagine any one engaged in a more beneficent course of action than a Viceroy of India who devotes all his talents and energy to the good of the people over whom he is set. In his case the benevolent despot is sure to be well chosen, and as his time is limited his country gets the best of his powers; his chances of going wrong are extremely small, whereas the good that he may do is difficult to measure. Democratic governments have generally been found strong in the control of dependencies, and democratic England is no exception to this rule.

The Indian Civil Service was no creation of a human brain; it has grown up gradually and has been evolved as circumstances required it. It has got rid of its defects and enhanced its merits, until it stands to-day as the most perfectly wise and virtuous bureaucracy which the world has ever seen. Those who travel in India find Englishmen and Englishwomen at their very best. A corrupt or self-seeking civil servant is a thing unknown; if he sins, it is rather through ignorance and lack of imagination or excess of zeal than through the traditions of routine. The responsibility with which a civil servant is invested the moment he arrives in India steadies and strengthens his character; the weak and self-indulgent are sobered by the serious nature of their work and by the healthiness of the moral atmosphere which they breathe. It has been said that no nation but England has sufficient political stability to place a subject in the position of a Viceroy of India; and certainly no nation but England could furnish so accomplished and trustworthy a Civil Service, so ready for all tasks and so capable of performing them. At a university a man gains a reputation not so much by knowing anything as by its being perfectly certain that he knows nothing else. But in India versatility is admired for its own sake, and the present Viceroy owes much of his reputation to the fact that he can deal in a masterly manner with a great variety of subjects. I express no opinion about the natives, because I was not sufficiently long with them to form a judgment. They seemed to be very well treated by their English masters, and they are undoubtedly deeply attached to the English Raj.

My last words shall be of a miscellaneous character. Put on your helmet as soon as you enter the Canal, and wear it whenever the sun shines, except in the cool of the evening. Take a warm bath twice a day, before breakfast and before dinner. Remember that cold is more dangerous than heat, and that the greatest of all evils is a chill. It may render you helpless in a few minutes, and death in India gives but a short shrift. Drink no water unless it is boiled and filtered, and no milk that you cannot trust. Remember that cholera may lurk in jellies, blancmanges, and salads, and that you can never know through what bag the one may have been strained or with what water the other may have been washed. Eat no fruit after the middle of the day, and beware of shellfish. In the cool season the same clothes are worn as in an English summer, and it is useless to burden yourself with white suits which you will never put on, and which would excite ridicule if you did. Do not walk about with a white umbrella, unless you wish to stamp yourself as a globe-trotter. Society in India is punctilious, and the observance of social rules is more strictly enforced than with us. These are trivial matters, but life is made up of trivialities, and a happy holiday in India is cheaply purchased by a little forethought. Once experience the force of that life-giving sun, the parent of health and energy, and thought, and you will always be longing to bask again in the full effulgence of its beams.

THE END